THE TRIUMPH
of GOODNESS

Text copyright © Lisa Cherrett 2003
The author asserts the moral right
to be identified as the author of this work

Published by
The Bible Reading Fellowship
First Floor, Elsfield Hall
15–17 Elsfield Way, Oxford OX2 8FG

ISBN 1 84101 308 0
First published 2003
10 9 8 7 6 5 4 3 2 1 0
All rights reserved

Acknowledgments

Unless otherwise stated, scripture quotations are taken from the *Holy Bible, New International Version*, copyright © 1973, 1978, 1984 by International Bible Society, are used by permission of Hodder & Stoughton Limited. All rights reserved. 'NIV' is a registered trademark of International Bible Society. UK trademark number 1448790.

Scripture quotations taken from The New Revised Standard Version of the Bible, Anglicized Edition, copyright © 1989, 1995 by the Division of Christian Education of the National Council of the Churches of Christ in the USA, are used by permission. All rights reserved.

The following words/phrases are proprietary names or are registered in the United Kingdom or as European Community trademarks:
Albus Dumbledore; Draco Malfoy; Frodo Baggins; Gilderoy Lockhart; Gollum; Hagrid; Harry Potter; Harry Potter and the Chamber of Secrets; Harry Potter and the Goblet of Fire; Harry Potter and the Order of the Phoenix; Harry Potter and the Philosopher's Stone; Harry Potter and the Prisoner of Azkaban; Hermione Granger; Hogsmeade; Hogwarts; The Lord of the Rings; The Lord of the Rings: The Fellowship of the Ring; The Lord of the Rings: The Return of the King; Lord Voldemort; Muggles; Ron Weasley; Sirius Black; Tom Riddle; Star Wars; Star Wars: The Return of the Jedi

A catalogue record for this book is available from the British Library

Printed and bound in Great Britain by
Bookmarque, Croydon

THE TRIUMPH
of GOODNESS

BIBLICAL THEMES IN THE HARRY POTTER STORIES

LISA CHERRETT

ABBREVIATIONS USED IN THIS BOOK

PS   *Harry Potter and the Philosopher's Stone*
CoS *Harry Potter and the Chamber of Secrets*
PoA *Harry Potter and the Prisoner of Azkaban*
GoF *Harry Potter and the Goblet of Fire*
OoP *Harry Potter and the Order of the Phoenix*

*For my dad, Ron, whose numerous bedtime re-readings
of Susie Squirrel introduced me to the joys of literature;
for my mum, Gwendoline, whose 'Gentle Jesus…' prayers
dug a foundation for my faith; and for my husband, Chris,
who introduced me to Harry.*

CONTENTS

INTRODUCTION

One summer evening in 1999, my husband excitedly showed me three books he'd bought that day on the strength of a book review in a daily newspaper. Everyone was talking about this series, he told me, and he was sure we'd both enjoy reading them. They were the *Harry Potter* books by J.K. Rowling: *The Philosopher's Stone*, *The Chamber of Secrets* and *The Prisoner of Azkaban*.

Before very long, it was my turn to read *The Philosopher's Stone*, and by the time I'd reached the beginning of Chapter 2, I knew that I had discovered a new literary passion. Like many readers before and since, I was captivated by the three-dimensional 'reality' of the characters, the bubbling humour of the storytelling and a compelling need to know what was going to happen to the orphaned child left on the doorstep of number four Privet Drive, 'Harry Potter—the boy who lived!' As I read on through the saga, I was swept up into an outrageously creative world of exuberant joy, peopled by good, bad and indifferent characters for whom I felt real compassion, and in which events constantly took intriguing twists and turns before the mystery was finally revealed and evil defeated.

A year later, shortly after the publication of the fourth book in the series, *The Goblet of Fire*, I was staggered to discover on the Internet several articles by Christians in America claiming that the *Harry Potter* stories were demonically inspired and blasphemous, anti-family and anti-authority, full of blood and violence and satanic symbolism, promoting pagan worship, belief in reincarnation and communication with the dead, not to mention the vices of self-gain, revenge and dominance. These claims were in some cases 'supported' by short quotations from the books, taken out of context and twisted to mean something quite different from what I believed J.K. Rowling had originally intended. The dark world described by these critics bore no resemblance to the joyous one in which I had been immersed so recently.

Since then, the controversy has continued. Opinion is still divided among Christians about whether or not the *Harry Potter* stories are spiritually harmful. The concern is magnified by the fact that the books have sold in their millions worldwide, appear to be addictive (many people claim to read them over and over again) and are eagerly devoured by children even as young as seven or eight years of age.

Personally I have yet to read any criticism of the *Harry Potter* stories that convinces me they have an evil, corrupting influence or promote interest in occult practice. Neither do I believe that they are 'Christian' literature in the way that C.S. Lewis' *Narnia Chronicles* evidently are. However, my own approach to the stories is strongly informed by Lewis' literary theory, especially as it relates to the influence of classic 'myth'.

C.S. Lewis observes that literature written by non-Christian authors may contain what he calls 'sub-Christian' elements—values that are not distinctively Christian but reach some way towards the unique body of ideas that make up Christian doctrine. Lewis goes on to suggest that these sub-Christian values are, of course, a step backwards for the already convinced Christian but may (although not necessarily) point uncommitted readers in the direction of Christian belief. As an example, he cites the poetry of Wordsworth. William Wordsworth (1770–1850) was definitely not a Christian poet: his work is full of pantheism—the belief that God resides and may be worshipped in every element of the natural world. However, Lewis argues:

For some souls I believe, for my own I remember, Wordsworthian contemplation can be the first and lowest form of recognition that there is something outside ourselves which demands reverence. To return to Pantheistic errors about the nature of this something would, for a Christian, be very bad. But... for 'the man coming up from below' the Wordsworthian experience is an advance. Even if he goes no further he has escaped the worst arrogance of materialism: if he goes on he will be converted.[1]

Lewis himself claimed that the pagan myths he had loved from his early years eventually pointed him to Christ. Closer to our own day, David Wilkinson, Christian author of *The Power of the Force: The spirituality of the Star Wars films*, witnesses that his reading of the *Star Wars* novel as a non-Christian teenager helped to spark the realization that 'there was more to life than just what we see; there is hope, and evil is real'.[2]

So, for the person who knows nothing of the Christian gospel, sub-Christian literary themes can capture the imagination and provide a foothold for the gospel in that person's mind, if he or she is ever fortunate enough to hear it at a later date.

My own Christian conversion came at the early age of 11 and was grounded mainly in the teaching I received in my local church and Sunday school from the age of 5. However, my reading of secular literature has played an important role in my ongoing discipleship, throwing up all kinds of ideas to be compared and contrasted with biblical wisdom. It has often provided insights into Christian ways of thinking that I would not have gained from reading the Bible alone. For example, at the age of 13, a children's book by Penelope Lively, *The Driftway*,[3] impressed on me the infinite value of the individual, long before I understood the biblical concept that we are all created unique, in the image of God, and before I noticed the respect with which Jesus treated those whom others rejected. Similarly, *Watership Down*, by Richard Adams,[4] shows a model of servant leadership in a fictional rabbit community, which helped me to understand the Christian concept that greatness does not come from superior size, strength or brainpower. As far as I'm aware, neither Penelope Lively nor Richard Adams has publicly affirmed a Christian faith, but this did not hinder me from learning something about God's ways through their work.

Since those early teenage years, when I realized that all the finest, most captivating literature deals with the big issues—the 'religious' issues of life and death, good and evil, and the forces that build and destroy relationships between people—the interaction between my Christian faith and my love of literature has been of immense importance to me. Indeed, these two most deep-rooted aspects of my thought life have developed and grown together side by side, nourishing one another.

It is second nature to me to read a work of literature or watch a film and consider how the ideas within the story compare and contrast with Christian thinking, to wonder what the author's views on faith are and to explore the ideas further in the context of biblical study. Specific biblical imagery appears sometimes in the most surprising of literary contexts. For example, at the climax to the film *The Terminator* (which I watched only to humour a friend), the seemingly unstoppable evil robot is finally destroyed by having its head crushed, just after having reached out to grasp the heroine's heel. The words of Genesis 3:15 leapt to my mind as soon as I saw the event on screen—but I have no idea whether or not this was a deliberate allusion on the part of the film maker.

It was natural, therefore, when I fell in love with the *Harry Potter* stories, for me to think about how the themes of the story related to Christian belief—for my own amusement and to develop my own personal faith. My response to the story would probably have remained personal had it not been for the very public hostility that J.K. Rowling's writings have aroused among some Christians. I was motivated to write this book initially out of grief, shame and anger at the ways in which the *Harry Potter* books have been, in my view, misrepresented by certain sections of the Church, and I felt that my starkly contrasting view needed to be expressed to a wider audience to redress the balance. Yet these negative emotions would not have been robust enough on their own to sustain my writing of this book. Instead, as I have studied the issues involved more deeply, I have been inspired afresh simply by the excitement of the interplay between the two loves of my life—first, the revelation of God in Jesus Christ, and, second, secular literature.

It would be foolish to claim that the *Harry Potter* stories are intended to be Christian parallels or that any of the details of the plots are directly inspired by biblical ideas. The God of the Bible is not acknowledged in them; the Christian festivals of Christmas and

Easter are celebrated at Hogwarts School in a merely secular fashion; and, unlike in the *Narnia Chronicles*, there is no one specific Christ-figure who acts as a sinless redeemer for a sinner or group of sinners. Moreover, the books are almost completely devoid of Christian symbolism: the lion and snake (depicted on the cover of this book), symbols of Gryffindor and Slytherin houses respectively, are the only pictures that have any conceivable parallel in biblical imagery. Nonetheless, I believe that the stories do contain a multitude of sub-Christian values, while many of their themes and events might serve to provoke deeper thought about aspects of Christian doctrine for people like me who have an existing Christian commitment.

Is it important, though, for us to identify and analyse 'sub-Christian' ideas in secular literature? Surely we should be attempting to guard the truth of the gospel, especially where younger generations are involved? In most cases where Christian commentators have expressed criticism of the *Harry Potter* stories, they have majored on the need to 'protect our children' from a perceived threat to their spiritual well-being—and by 'our children' they mean children from Christian families who are part of a wider Christian community, the Church.

Of course it is right and proper that parents should seek to protect their children from influences that might harm them. Naturally, many Christian parents fear that their children might abandon the faith and be led into lifestyles that fall short of the standards of the kingdom of God. In the increasingly difficult job of parenting, it is vital for those who find themselves faced with this heavy responsibility to follow their consciences and lead their families in ways that they personally feel are honouring to God. However, the stark fact is that the vast majority of the tens of thousands of readers of the *Harry Potter* books in the UK alone are not 'our children' in this sense. They are people who are outside the community of the Church and, in very many cases, outside the Church because it has never invited them in. As the apostle Paul puts it, '... how are they to believe in one of whom they have never heard? And how are they to hear without someone to proclaim him?' (Romans 10:14, NRSV).

My focus in this book is principally on the effect of the *Harry Potter* stories on these numerous readers (of every age, not only children) who are outside the Church. Among the younger generations especially (by which I mean people up to the age of about 30), complete ignorance of the basic doctrines of Christianity and the once-famous Old Testament stories is at an unprecedented level. Evangelists can no longer assume any foundations of knowledge on which to base their communication of the gospel. For this reason, I believe that we in the Church urgently need to give up the siege mentality that focuses exclusively on self-preservation, look outwards and use every opportunity to engage with people who are not yet believers. To return to C.S. Lewis, in the first book of his 'cosmic trilogy', *Out of the Silent Planet*, he puts into his hero's mouth the words, 'What we need for the moment is not so much a body of belief as a body of people familiarized with certain ideas'.[5] I am convinced that the *Harry Potter* stories have the potential to produce 'a body of people familiarized with certain ideas' that can re-lay a foundation for Christian faith. If this is true, we cannot afford to ignore the opportunities for outreach that might be provided by this literary phenomenon.

I should stress again that I do not claim that author J.K. Rowling set out to include sub-Christian values in her work or to write a tale with a deliberate specific 'moral' in mind. Neither have I strained to read Christian ideas into the stories in order to justify my love of them. The *Harry Potter* books are, first and foremost, fantasy stories to enjoy, so no apologies or excuses are necessary if we simply enjoy them. For me, however, a significant part of my enjoyment of the story is that I find echoes there of the character of the God I know and love. In the chapters that follow, I aim to trace those echoes to their source and suggest ways in which they might point others to God.

I would like at this stage to explain a little more about the way in which I have approached the subject matter in this book. Chapters 2 to 6 each take a major biblical theme and first compare the viewpoint of scripture with the assumptions of our secular postmodern society with regard to that theme. They go on to show how, in each case, the *Harry Potter* stories express ideas that come far closer to reflecting the biblical view than the contemporary secular slant on the issue. The final chapter is a challenge to the Church to engage fully with society and outlines some ways in which I believe we have fallen short of that aim, especially with regard to the phenomenon that is the *Harry Potter* series.

There is something particular to bear in mind about each of the three elements in the comparison. First, all of the biblical themes that I've chosen are enormous fields of study in their own right—whole books of theology could be written on each one. It has therefore been impossible for me to provide an exhaustive account of each theme within the space of half a chapter. I have attempted only to give a balanced overview, focusing on the essence of the topic as suggested by both Old and New Testaments, but with a special emphasis on the teaching and example of Jesus Christ. Having said that, there is a fair amount of biblical study in most chapters, so please be patient—the analysis of the *Harry Potter* stories does appear eventually!

Second, it is important for me to give a warning about my treatment of the *Harry Potter* books themselves. Each one is a mystery story, with a strong 'whodunnit?' element and many secrets ingeniously hidden within the plot. My comments on the stories in the chapters to come will reveal many of these secrets, including the hidden identities of the various villains and the much-hyped 'major death' in *The Order of the Phoenix*. These 'spoilers' have been unavoidable, but I would hate to ruin anyone's enjoyment of the *Harry Potter* books as a result. If you have not yet read all five of the books and intend to do so, you may wish to put this book aside until you have discovered for yourself exactly 'whodunnit' in them all.

Third, my descriptions of postmodern attitudes to the biblical values under discussion are almost entirely negative in their conclusions. However, I am aware that there are aspects of postmodern experience that in themselves provide fertile ground for the growth of Christian faith. The search for true community in our contemporary fragmented society is something that could be satisfied by a demonstration of 'church' as a network of genuinely loving relationships. The revival of interest in storytelling (personal narratives as opposed to 'metanarratives') means that personal testimony and the imaginative retelling of Bible stories and parables might prove to be ever more fruitful methods of evangelism, while the general openness to the spiritual dimension, as opposed to a purely rational mindset, means that Christianity is likely to be more readily embraced as an ongoing relationship with God than as a rigid belief system to which intellectual assent needs to be given. In the context of the major biblical themes covered in this book, though, the postmodernist rejection of the existence of 'absolutes' comes very much to the fore. Indeed, it is this characteristic that most often brings the contemporary worldview into conflict with the Bible on these issues.

So, what are the sub-Christian elements to be found in the *Harry Potter* stories? I would suggest that some of the most important are personal choice, hope, grace, truth, power, authority and the ways in which evil is overcome by goodness. All of these values will be discussed in the chapters that follow, but, first, it is necessary to tackle the superficially obvious reason for many Christians' disapproval of the stories—the fact that they involve something called 'witchcraft'.

CHAPTER 1

WITCHCRAFT IN THE
HARRY POTTER STORIES

Many Christian attacks on the *Harry Potter* stories hinge on the claim that the books are 'about witchcraft'. Perhaps it is natural to assume (particularly if one has not actually read the books!) that because Harry is described as a wizard and attends 'Hogwarts School of Witchcraft and Wizardry', the stories are based on occult belief and practice, made all the more dangerous to susceptible minds because of the highly entertaining nature of the narrative. This assumption leads to the fear that readers of the *Harry Potter* books will be encouraged to pursue an interest in real-life occultism as a result of becoming immersed in the world of the story. Are these claims actually true? Are the *Harry Potter* books 'about witchcraft' and do they promote an interest in real occult practice?

Deuteronomy 18:10–11 says, 'Let no one be found among you who sacrifices his son or daughter in the fire, who practises divination or sorcery, interprets omens, engages in witchcraft, or casts spells, or who is a medium or spiritist or who consults the dead.' This is a clear basis for Christian belief that involvement in witchcraft of any sort is forbidden by God and therefore must be dangerous to human well-being. I agree fully with this position: 'witchcraft' is out of bounds to followers of Christ. What, though, does 'witchcraft' actually mean? We would assume that in Deuteronomy the writer is talking about an activity that involves contact with an evil spiritual realm with the aim of controlling the natural world in a supernatural way. This is not what the word 'witchcraft' means when it is used in the context of the *Harry Potter* stories.

American author and former politician Charles Colson has hit the nail squarely on the head with his comment that the witchcraft involved in the stories is 'purely mechanical, as opposed to occultic'.[6] Occult activities as we know of them in the real world are, of course, intimately concerned with the supernatural realm. We live in a natural world governed by scientific laws—the laws of physics and chemistry. Those who engage in occult, supernatural practices reach over, as it were, into a separate spiritual realm in order to gain powers that are beyond the natural world. In the fictional world of the *Harry Potter* stories, this is not the way things work. Harry and his friends do not derive their magic powers from a spiritual dimension outside of their natural environment. Their whole environment is governed by natural laws that are different from those in our real world: portraits and photographs move and speak; staircases lead somewhere different on Fridays; it's possible to turn beetles into coat buttons, and hedgehogs into pincushions; there are unicorns and centaurs in the forest and merpeople in the lake. So, within the world of this story, Harry's powers are entirely natural—unrelated to the supernatural world that we believe to exist in reality.

It is made clear at several points in the *Harry Potter* stories that in this fictional wizarding world, magic is a replacement for scientific technology—it is the means by which the wizards manipulate and control their physical environment. In *The Goblet of Fire*, Hermione talks about 'all those substitutes for magic Muggles use—electricity, and computers and radar, and all those things...' (pp. 475–476), while Arthur Weasley, on being told how a telephone works, comments, '*Ingenious*, really, how many ways Muggles have found of getting along without magic' (*CoS*, p. 37).

So, when the good and evil wizards all use the same magical power in their battles with each other, the equivalent conflict in the real world is not between supernatural 'white magic' and 'black magic', both of which Christians believe to be forbidden by the Bible. Rather, the comparison is with the kinds of technology listed by Hermione, all of which are, in themselves, morally neutral sources of power. Electricity can be used in a controlled manner to heat and light our homes; it can also be used as a method of torture. (Unharnessed, of course, it is highly dangerous.) Similarly, Internet technology can provide opportunities for the storage and exchange of useful information; it can also be used to spread pornography. Radar is employed by aircraft to aid navigation for peaceful purposes; it can also be used to guide weapons of destruction to their targets. The sources of power are neither good nor bad in themselves; the use to which that power is put may be good or bad, depending on the moral choice made by the human beings controlling it.

Alan Jacobs, Professor of English at Wheaton College, USA, suggests that the *Harry Potter* series should, in fact, challenge us to show more concern about the use of science in the real world, which affects each and every one of us profoundly. In his article, 'Harry Potter's Magic', he writes, 'The technocrats of this world hold in their hands powers almost infinitely greater than those of Albus Dumbledore and Voldemort: how worried are we about them, and their influence over our children? Not worried enough, I would say.'[7] Jacobs is quite right: J.K. Rowling's imaginative description of schoolchildren magically transforming matchsticks into needles should be of far less concern to Christians than, say, the ethical issues surrounding advances in genetic engineering.

This brings me to my next point, which is that a very large proportion of the magic performed by Harry and his friends is utterly absurd—it is all impossible in our real world. For example, in *The Goblet of Fire*, Neville Longbottom has a particularly difficult time in Transfiguration class and ends up 'accidentally transplanting his own ears onto a cactus', while Fred and George Weasley enchant custard creams for fun, so that anyone eating one turns temporarily into a large canary. The magic wands that are necessary for the performance of controlled magic are hollow wooden sticks of varying lengths, each containing a unicorn hair or a dragon heartstring or a phoenix tail-feather. (Other magic substances are sometimes used, but these three are favoured by the supplier of wands to most Hogwarts students.) Obviously, unicorns, dragons and phoenixes are imaginary beasts, so the very means of performing Harry Potter's kind of 'witchcraft' are non-existent in reality.

Apart from the simple occurrence of the word 'witchcraft', however, there are several specific criticisms that are often made by J.K. Rowling's detractors regarding the supposed occult content of the stories. It is only fair to treat these concerns seriously, as they are raised time and time again in anti-Potter writings. However, as I am about to show, they are often based on quotations from the books that are taken out of context and then misinterpreted with no regard for the underlying ethos of the text, or on sweeping generalizations that can very easily be rebutted. Other criticisms relating to the over-all moral tone of the books and the ethical and spiritual values that they promote (for example, issues to do with respect for authority, revenge and mercy, self-gain and self-sacrifice) will be addressed under separate headings in the chapters still to come.

DEATH: THE NEXT GREAT ADVENTURE

A very common criticism relating to occultism is that the stories promote witchcraft beliefs about the afterlife and contact with the dead. For the critics, one of the most offensive sentences in the four *Harry Potter* books so far published is spoken by Headmaster Albus Dumbledore to Harry on p. 215 of *The Philosopher's Stone*: '... to the well-organised mind, death is but the next great adventure.' Some commentators quote these words without any analysis at all, as if readers are supposed to realize immediately how diabolical the idea is. One, however, an unnamed spokesman for 'Freedom Village USA', states that Dumbledore is advocating a Wiccan doctrine that after death the soul grows young again in preparation for reincarnation.[8]

What other devilish ideas might we imagine are being promoted by the Professor in the words 'death is but the next great adventure'? Is he encouraging suicide, for example? Or are the critics merely concerned that he fails to mention the possibility of judgment after death by an all-knowing, holy God?

In fact, when these twelve words are read in the context of the whole book, it becomes clear that Professor Dumbledore is speaking about a man who has had a long and productive life and is preparing to die at a very ripe age (665, to be exact). He is simply reassuring Harry that natural death is nothing to fear if one has achieved one's life's work and is well prepared to leave this world behind. He is saying nothing more sinister than that and his words are certainly not carrying any suggestion of the possibility of reincarnation. It would surely be remarkable if Dumbledore went on to expound the gospel message that the only way to be prepared for death is to believe in the saving grace of Jesus Christ, which allows us to face judgment without fear! Would we seriously expect a fictional character in any other secular novel to do so?

The related claim that the *Harry Potter* books condone deliberate contact with the dead is equally ill-founded. We learn from the story that Harry's parents, Lily and James, died when Harry was exactly 15 months old. From the moment Harry discovers the true circumstances of their deaths at the hands of the evil wizard, Lord Voldemort, they become an important part of his emotional life and appear in some form in books 1, 3, 4 and 5 of the series. Nevertheless, these appearances emphatically do not represent the spirits of James and Lily Potter. Even in *The Goblet of Fire*, where images of James and Lily actually speak to Harry, it is made explicit that the figures are not the spirits of his parents—they are 'echoes' of the spells used by Voldemort to kill them. Furthermore, there are two specific occasions in the saga when it is made clear that attempting contact with his parents or even dwelling on their memory would be detrimental to Harry's well-being.

First, in *The Philosopher's Stone*, Harry discovers a magic mirror that reflects the deepest desire of one's heart. In it he sees himself surrounded by his mother, father and other dead members of his family. Professor Dumbledore, knowing that Harry is starting to make a habit of visiting the mirror, advises him thus:

This mirror will give us neither knowledge or truth. Men have wasted away before it, entranced by what they have seen, or been driven mad, not knowing if what it shows is real or even possible. The Mirror will be moved to a new home tomorrow, Harry, and I ask you not to go looking for it again... It does not do to dwell on dreams and forget to live, remember that' (PS, p. 157).

Second, in *The Prisoner of Azkaban*, Harry is repeatedly forced to relive a vivid babyhood memory of his parents' last moments, in which he distinctly hears his father's voice and his mother's screams. A teacher gives him special instruction on how to combat this disturbing memory, but Harry realizes that he half wants to keep hearing his parents' voices and that this desire is preventing him from learning the lesson properly. Harry therefore takes himself in hand: '"They're dead," he told himself sternly. "They're dead, and listening to echoes of them won't bring them back. You'd better get a grip on yourself..."' (p. 180).

The death of his parents is not the only bereavement that Harry has to face. In *The Order of the Phoenix*, after the demise of his god-father Sirius Black at the hands of Bellatrix Lestrange, Harry is sorely tempted to try to make contact with him by means of a magic two-way mirror given to him by Sirius earlier in the story. But the mirror refuses to respond; Sirius is unreachable, and Harry is forced to accept that he will not see his godfather again during his own lifetime.

So the accusation that the *Harry Potter* books encourage the raising of dead spirits is quite false. On the contrary, they strongly suggest that any attempt to do so will prove neither possible nor beneficial.

POTIONS

What are we to make of the following speech by Professor Severus Snape, Potions master at Hogwarts School, quoted by Berit Kjos in the article 'Bewitched by Harry Potter'[9] as an example of dangerous occult ideas being promoted by the *Harry Potter* stories?

I don't expect you will really understand the beauty of the softly simmering cauldron with its shimmering fumes, the delicate power of liquids that creep through human veins, bewitching the mind, ensnaring the senses...

Professor Snape's introduction to the study of Potions sounds enticingly sinister in this brief snippet of 34 words from page 102 of *The Philosopher's Stone*. Reading this quotation out of context might easily lead one to assume that Snape's students (and the real-life readers of the book) would be deeply impressed by his speech and ravenously eager to start 'bewitching the mind' and 'ensnaring the senses' with their newfound occult skills. It has even been suggested by some Christians that young people are being seduced into drug-taking by such words.

As the story progresses, however, it becomes clear that Potions is one of the least popular subjects on the curriculum for Harry and his friends (Harry hates it) and Professor Snape is far from being a well-respected teacher (witness Ron Weasley's tongue-in-cheek muttered comment in *The Chamber of Secrets*: 'D'you think we've got nothing better to do in Potions than listen to Snape?', p. 120). Snape hopes to impress his new class of first-years with his superior knowledge—to awe them into submission. Yet, what kind of supernatural mind-altering drug does the class actually brew up after Snape's speech here? 'A simple potion to cure boils' is the answer. The humorous irony is obvious when the context is considered. Given Snape's vindictive temperament and the difficulty of the subject he teaches, the lingering impression in the series as a whole is that the 'beauty of the softly simmering cauldron' is nothing but a bad joke.

DIVINATION

Another specific criticism with regard to the 'occultism' in the *Harry Potter* books is that they describe and encourage the practice of divination—or all kinds of fortune-telling. It is true that Hogwarts students in the third year and upwards attend Divination lessons. However, Christian critics of this aspect of the *Harry Potter* stories always fail to mention the fact that these lessons are 'taught' (if that is the correct word) by a woman, Professor Sybill Trelawney, who is widely acknowledged to be a fraud, and that J.K. Rowling undermines the credibility of the subject itself at every opportunity.

Hermione Granger, one of Harry's best friends, comments after her first Divination class, 'That lesson was absolute rubbish...' (*PoA*, p. 85). In fact, Hermione makes a permanent exit from Divination halfway through the year, in utter disgust at its futility. Harry and Ron persist, but learn nothing at all in their classes. In *The Goblet of Fire*, they abandon any serious attempt at their homework and resort to 'the old Divination standby... make it up' (p. 195). Professor McGonagall, the sensible, no-nonsense Deputy Head, makes no effort to hide her contempt for the subject. Her response to Professor Trelawney's display of superstitious fear during a Christmas dinner in *The Prisoner of Azkaban* is to pass her a dish of food with the words, 'Tripe, Sybill?' (p. 170). The centaurs of the Forbidden Forest, such as Firenze, do believe in the power of astrology to reveal 'great tides of evil or change' (*OoP*, p. 531), but Firenze is at pains to insist that even his kind sometimes read the signs wrongly. So the reader of the *Harry Potter* stories is left under no illusion, from respected students and teachers alike, that palmistry, tea-leaf reading, crystal-ball gazing and astrology, along with superstition and omens, are unreliable, boring, useless and a complete waste of time and energy.

It is also worth noting that J.K. Rowling shows a commitment to the idea of personal choice and responsibility in the *Harry Potter* stories that rules out belief in divination as a powerful means of foretelling our destiny. If our futures are shaped by our own deliberate choices, they cannot be determined by the movement of the planets, the pattern of leaves in the bottom of a teacup or the particular arrangement of fog in a crystal ball. We see this principle first in Chapter 15 of *The Philosopher's Stone*, where Firenze rejects even his own belief in astrology as a guide for his behaviour, acting against the 'advice' of the planets and his fellow centaurs in order to rescue Harry from the evil that threatens him in the Forbidden Forest. Then, in Chapter 37 of *The Order of the Phoenix*, Professor Dumbledore explains that even the fulfilment of the lost prophecy concerning Harry and Lord Voldemort depended on a choice made by Voldemort—the choice to attack Harry rather than Neville Longbottom (see *OoP*, p. 742). (See the next chapter for more on the importance of personal moral choice in the books.)

This body of evidence that fortune-telling and related occult activities are not condoned in the stories means that when a Christian critic whispers, 'Harry Potter learns Divination, you know!' he or she is not quite telling the whole truth.

MUGGLES AND WIZARDS

There is a common assumption that J.K. Rowling's depiction of Muggles (non-wizards) in her story is intended to be a veiled attack on Christians and others who reject occult practice. Berit Kjos' article, mentioned previously, defines Muggles as 'those boring, blinded, and biased humans who either don't believe in the world of witches or who despise it as evil'. It goes on to say, 'Harry's cruel aunt and uncle fit the last category. And, from Harry's point of view, so would you if you see witchcraft as dangerous and demonic.' This is a serious misunderstanding.

A simple, factual, non-emotive definition of a Muggle is simply this: 'a human being in the fantasy world of the *Harry Potter* books who is not born a wizard'. In the books, people are either born wizards or they are born Muggles. There is no choice in the matter, and 'Muggle' is a morally neutral term. Harry's 'cruel uncle and aunt' are not cruel because they're Muggles, they're cruel because they're selfish and fearful. They both believe in the wizarding world and they never give any indication that they think it's evil. Aunt Petunia rejects Harry's magical world because she was jealous of the attention her sister (Harry's mother) received when she first started at Hogwarts school: '... for my mother and father... it was Lily this and Lily that...' she explains (PS, p. 44). Uncle Vernon's rejection is based on his fear and hatred of 'anything strange or mysterious', not any conviction that Harry's 'abnormality', as he calls it, is morally wrong.

Furthermore, not all Muggles are pictured in the stories as cruel, selfish and narrow-minded. Hermione Granger's parents are portrayed as perfectly respectable professional people and Frank Bryce, the gardener who confronts Voldemort in Chapter 1 of *Goblet of Fire*, is courageous, dignified and public-spirited. Also, as we shall see in the next chapters of this book, not all of the wizards who feature in the story are admirable. It certainly is not the case that J.K. Rowling intends to portray non-wizards as 'boring, blinded and biased' while showcasing supposedly 'occult' practitioners as shining examples of virtue.

FEAR AND EVIL

Related to these concerns about the supposed presentation of occult belief and practice is the charge that the portrayal of evil within the books is too terrifying for young, impressionable minds. Fear is, indeed, a debilitating emotion when it takes hold of a person, and certain aspects of the *Harry Potter* stories (most notably, in my opinion, the Dementors and the revival of Lord Voldemort), can be frightening. Fear is a universal emotion, however, that we all have to face at some time in our lives, and with good reason—the world is not always a safe and pleasant place in which to live. 'Face' is the key word here: fears increase when we try to sweep them under the carpet and diminish when we confront them head-on. In fact, this truth is expressed in *The Prisoner of Azkaban*, when Harry and his classmates are taught in Defence Against the Dark Arts (DADA) classes how to defeat their greatest imagined fear—by staring it in the face and laughing at it (Chapter 7, 'The Boggart in the Wardrobe').

J.K. Rowling's own answer to this criticism of her work has been heard in several interviews, including one with Evan Solomon of *CBC Newsround* on 18 July 2000. She argues that she has a moral obligation to show that Voldemort's evil is a genuinely serious thing, to be opposed wholeheartedly: he is not just a 'pantomime villain', scary-looking but harmless really. The contrast between good and evil then becomes stark: Voldemort's extreme evil highlights Dumbledore's extreme goodness, while the fear that Voldemort inspires shows up the true quality of Harry's courage. Rowling's intuition (which is in line with Christian thought) has been borne out by her readers' reactions. I heard of one young teenage girl, for example, who thought Voldemort was 'cool', until he murdered her favourite character in *The Goblet of Fire*. Then she realized just how destructive and repulsive evil really is. This realization was surely an advance in that child's moral development.

DO THE BOOKS PROMOTE INTEREST IN OCCULTISM?

It appears that some Christians—especially Christian parents and teachers—are worried that young and impressionable readers of the *Harry Potter* books will become so absorbed in the imaginative, magical world of the story that they will be drawn to experiment with real witchcraft in an attempt to live out the excitement of Hogwarts School. Of course, the only reliable way to test this fear would be to conduct a controlled scientific study, but it is unlikely that such a study will ever be carried out. This means that anecdotal evidence—stories of people known to individuals—is the only kind that we will ever hear about, and such evidence can only ever be subjective.

I contribute regularly to a lively discussion forum on one of the many *Harry Potter* websites. Over a period of five months after the publication of *The Goblet of Fire*, in which over a thousand separate discussion topics were introduced, I witnessed just two occasions when 'real' witchcraft came up in the conversation. If it is true that exposure to the *Harry Potter* stories increases interest in the occult, I would expect that these readers—'hard-core', passionate *Harry Potter* fans aged 13 and upwards, who have re-read the books countless times and know them intimately—would be clamouring to contribute to debate on occult themes. In fact, nothing could be further from the truth. In one of these two cases, the introduction of 'real' witchcraft stopped the discussion dead and the topic disappeared from view a day later. In the other case, a few comments were made, all of them claiming disinterest or positive opposition to occultism and that discussion petered out within the week.

My own experience is that reading the *Harry Potter* stories has never, in any way, increased my desire to learn more about witchcraft or any other kind of occultism. To my alarm, however, when I first read Christian commentaries on the books claiming that they contained pagan symbolism, I caught myself thinking, 'Where is all this pagan symbolism, then? Perhaps I'd better buy a book on paganism to see if I can find out more.' Since then, I have seen the emergence of Christian 'experts' on witchcraft who have been educating the Church on the content of genuine occult practice, supposedly with the aim of exposing the roots of the fantasy magic found in the *Harry Potter* stories. Richard Abanes, writer of *Harry Potter and the Bible*[10] is probably the best-known example of such an author.

The irony is that while these witchcraft experts and their followers have been immersing their minds in occultism, genuine Potter fans have been happily speculating on such questions as 'Will Ron and Hermione's friendship really blossom into romance?' or 'What is the source of Harry's inherited wealth?' or 'Did Hagrid ever give back Sirius Black's motorbike and, if not, where is it now?' I wonder who is being led astray here—the Potter fans fascinated by character and plot developments or those well-intentioned Christians who are rejecting storybook magic in favour of real knowledge of occultism.

It would be most regrettable if the warnings against reading the *Harry Potter* books actually encouraged people as innocent as myself to become knowledgeable about the content of occult belief. However, I can easily understand how such an outcome might occur.

The two books I mentioned in the Introduction—*The Driftway* and *Watership Down*—both contain elements that might be considered occultic in nature. Once again, however, although both of these books had a profound impact on me as a young teenager, neither of them influenced me to explore the occult realm. *The Driftway* is based on a young boy's encounters with ghosts on an old country road in the Midlands, but it never occurred to me to go ghost-hunting along the roads around my Midlands childhood home. One of the central characters in *Watership Down* is clairvoyant, and saves his fellow rabbits from death on at least two occasions by means of his uncanny ability to 'see' danger ahead. This did not inspire me to consult a clairvoyant and I still intend never to do so.

My overriding interest in both of these books was in the developing relationships between the characters and the progression of the plot. As I have suggested above, exactly the same can be said of the experience of reading the *Harry Potter* books. My fellow contributors to our Internet discussion forum are wholly immersed in the characters and the twists and turns of the plot, producing wild and wonderful theories on how those elements are going to be developed in the books still to be published.

Of course, it may still be argued that even if the books themselves are harmless, their popularity is bound to lead to spin-offs that may be more damaging—books by other authors about child witches, for example, that will feed off the hype surrounding Harry. Indeed, there is a possibility that other authors will cash in on the 'magic' bandwagon. We need to remember, however, that the popularity of the *Harry Potter* books is due largely to their originality, so it is unlikely that a reader who loves Harry will be easily taken in by another author's poor imitation. The fact is that all of the other bestselling book series for children and young teenagers in recent months (such as Philip Pullman's *His Dark Materials* trilogy, *An Unfortunate Series of Events* by Lemony Snicket and *Artemis Fowl* by Eoin Colfer) have been distinctively different from J.K. Rowling's and are enjoyed for different reasons. It is not the case that a fan of the *Harry Potter* books will necessarily be interested in other books (or, indeed, TV shows such as *Sabrina the Teenage Witch*) that might be promoted to the same 'market'.

J.K. Rowling's stories affect many readers at very deep emotional levels, but it is simply nonsense to claim, as many critics do, that people are hooked on her stories because of the 'occult thrills' that they experience while reading about Harry's adventures. If asked why they love the books so passionately, many readers will talk about identifying with the very human joys, fears and tribulations of Harry and his friends, about the gloriously humorous dialogue, the unpredictable creativity of the storylines and the pleasure of observing new details with every re-reading. Only on my third reading of *The Prisoner of Azkaban* did I really notice Hermione Granger disappearing between lessons—something that is central to the subplot involving her overfull and exhausting timetable. A fifth reading of the same book made me aware that Professor Lupin is the only teacher who always calls students by their first names, which surely contributes to the very warm sympathy that most readers feel for him. These may seem insignificant details, but this rich, multilevel, imaginative and intellectual experience is what keeps fans coming back to the stories again and again, not any fascination with 'occult thrills'!

Further, I believe that there is something indefinable about the *Harry Potter* stories that inspires some readers on an even more profound level. They aspire to the wisdom of Professor Dumbledore, the loyalty of Hermione; they recognize and admire Harry's self-effacing nature and Hagrid's simple kindness; and they talk of being filled with a yearning for something beyond the humdrum material existence of everyday life, longing for a place where they really belong, with a truly loving community of friends. This is a far cry from the critics' assertions that the *Harry Potter* stories encourage lying, cheating and stealing. It seems far more likely to me that in a world where the glossy images of skin-deep beauty and spin-doctored values are all around us on the surface, the stories speak to their fans of a goodness that is fundamental, genuine, and long-lasting—something worth finding and keeping. In the following chapters, I shall explore some of the facets of that goodness.

CHAPTER 2

CHOICE AND DESTINY

*I have set before you life and death, blessings and curses.
Now choose life...*
DEUTERONOMY 30:19

*It is our choices, Harry, that show what we truly are,
far more than our abilities.*
HARRY POTTER AND THE CHAMBER OF SECRETS, P. 245

As consumers in a wealthy economy, we are probably more aware than ever before of the vast array of choices spread before us. Whether it be food, clothing, household goods, financial services or mobile phones, the options seem endless. We pride ourselves on being sophisticated enough to sift through all these many possibilities and make wise decisions about how best to gain value for money. Yet, when it comes to our ethical and moral behaviour, there is an increasing belief in society that our actions are determined by factors beyond our control. Pick up a tabloid newspaper and turn to the problem page. It's highly likely that you'll be able to read how a marriage has ended or an unwanted baby been conceived because 'the inevitable' happened between two people who found themselves inexplicably overcome by sexual desire. Watch a TV documentary on rising crime in deprived inner-city housing estates and hear the sad, empty-eyed children say, 'They don't give us anything to do, so we have to break windows, don't we?' In these expressions of helplessness, there is no recognition that we might choose to swim against the tide of circumstances, only a kind of bewilderment at the strength of the current.

As scientists discover more and more about the staggering complexity of our genetic make-up, they even consider the possibility that some people might be biologically 'wired' for aggression and criminal behaviour. In his book *Why Do They Do That?* Nick Pollard quotes Sir Michael Rutter's response to just such a suggestion in a 1996 report on 'Genetics of criminal and anti-social behaviour'. Sir Michael (child development expert from the Institute of Psychiatry) denied that genes lead people directly to commit criminal acts, but he continued:

There may be an increased... propensity to aggression or antisocial behaviour but whether or not the affected individual actually commits some criminal act will also be dependent on environmental predisposing factors or situational circumstances at the time.

Nick Pollard comments, 'Such scientists... may argue that our behaviour is determined by our genes, or by our environment, or by some combination of both. But none of them talks about free will, self-control or individual responsibility.'[11]

This refusal to recognize our freedom to choose between 'right' and 'wrong' might be seen as one strand of the worldview that we call postmodernism, in which all is relative, there are no overarching guiding principles that govern all our lives as human beings and no meaning to our existence apart from the fleeting pleasure or pain of the moment. It is very different in this respect from a worldview based on Judeo-Christian, biblical principles.

THE CENTRALITY OF FREE WILL

The Bible is a realistic collection of writings. It acknowledges the fact that we fallen human beings will instinctively blame others for our own misfortunes. In Genesis 3, for example, after eating the forbidden fruit, Adam wastes no time in accusing Eve rather than accepting responsibility for his deliberate disobedience, while Eve passes the buck straight on to the serpent; and the writer of Proverbs notices that 'One's own folly leads to ruin, yet the heart rages against the Lord' (Proverbs 19:3, NRSV). Such an approach to blame and responsibility can be observed in human life today, thousands of years down the line. However, in the moral guidelines they offer, the biblical writers have a more challenging vision. They seem quite adamant that our character and actions are ultimately determined by nothing other than our own heart, our own will, our own free choice.

The concept of free will is central to a Christian understanding of human nature, our relationship to God and the existence of evil in the world. We believe that God creates human beings with the freedom to choose whether or not to enter into a relationship with him and act in ways that please him. The fact that we sometimes choose to reject God causes him great personal pain, as we can see in the tears of Jesus, weeping over Jerusalem and crying out, 'O Jerusalem, Jerusalem... how often I have longed to gather your children together, as a hen gathers her chicks under her wings, but you were not willing!' (Luke 13:34). The results of disobedience to God can also be catastrophic to ourselves and other people, yet God still refuses to make us robots, programmed for obedience. Our free will is a precious gift from God, never to be undermined or violated, least of all by God himself.

CHARACTER BUILDING

Nevertheless, with freedom to choose comes personal responsibility for the outcome of our choices. This is the basis for the biblical idea that people can legitimately be held accountable for the consequences of their actions and may ultimately be judged by God for the good or evil choices they make in life. Even before the final judgment, though, the choices we make affect the kind of character that is moulded in us during our lifetime. C.S. Lewis recognized this principle of slow growth into good or evil character in his classic book *Mere Christianity*, in which he wrote:

Every time you make a choice you are turning the central part of you, the part that chooses, into something a little different from what it was before. And taking your life as a whole, with all your innumerable choices, all your life long you are slowly turning this central thing either into a heavenly creature or into a hellish creature.[12]

The assumption that people build good character gradually, by deliberately and repeatedly choosing good 'paths', and evil character by repeatedly choosing evil 'paths', underpins the whole of the book of Proverbs. This book in the Bible also suggests that the true quality of our character, whether basically good or bad, is shown up most clearly under the pressure of unpleasant or unexpected circumstances: 'When the storm has swept by, the wicked are gone, but the righteous stand firm for ever' (Proverbs 10:25).

Of course, Jesus made it clear that choosing and following good paths is not necessarily easy. In the Sermon on the Mount, he taught, '... wide is the gate and broad is the road that leads to destruction, and many enter through it. But small is the gate and narrow the road that leads to life, and only a few find it' (Matthew 7:13–14). The implication here is that people are likely to drift into evil unless they make a conscious decision to look for and find the good. We all know from our own experience that it's hard to do good when the wrong choice appears to offer us greater personal advantage. Lying is easier than telling the truth when a lie will get us out of trouble, and it is easier to respond to an insult with an outburst of anger than with gentleness and immediate forgiveness.

Jesus also recognized that people do not start life with equal advantages or opportunities, but suggested that this is not an excuse for fear, laziness or complacency in the choices we make. In his parable of the talents (Matthew 25:14–30), one man is given five pieces of silver, another is given two pieces and a third is given one piece. This rings true in our own experience: some people start life with rich parents, excellent opportunities in education, a pleasant living environment, all manner of entertainments and culturally enriching experiences; others have a few of these things, or none. However, the parable goes on to describe how the first two men succeed in investing and doubling their money, while the third buries his one piece in the ground and does nothing constructive with it. It is clear that some people 'bury' the advantages they are given and end up impoverished in character and achievements, while others boldly take hold of the smallest opportunity, grasp it firmly and multiply it. Again, C.S. Lewis endorses this principle: 'God does not judge [a man] on the raw material at all, but on what he has done with it.'[13]

DRIFT INTO EVIL

Given that we have both the freedom and responsibility to choose between good and bad paths in life, what factors are involved in steering us away from the good (more difficult) path and towards the bad (often easier) path? In the Anglican Prayer of Confession, worshippers admit that they have sinned against God and other people 'through negligence, through weakness, through [their] own deliberate fault', and these three categories do seem to encompass the vast majority of the choices we make for evil, whether those choices are relatively clear-sighted or the result of a 'drift' towards wrong behaviour.

Negligence implies a 'don't care' attitude, shown by a person who does not know and cannot be bothered to think seriously about the morality of their actions. Cain, with his unacceptable sacrifice to the Lord, had to be warned by God of the evil 'crouching at his door': he himself was blind to the danger. He took no notice of the warning, murdered his own brother, carelessly shrugged off the responsibility and then seemed shocked at the severity of his punishment (Genesis 4:4–14). Cain followed his own instincts and neglected to consider the power of that evil crouching so close to home until the terrible damage was done.

Most people, as the apostle Paul testified (Romans 7:19), know the good that they should do, but find themselves unable to do it because of weaknesses in their own nature. Consider Pilate, ordering the execution of an innocent man because he allowed political ambition to overcome his moral convictions (John 19:12–13), or Peter, losing courage and denying Jesus not just once but three times as soon as he felt his physical safety threatened (Luke 22:54–60). Many of the sinful actions recorded in the Bible and in our own experience can be put down to weakness of some sort, particularly fear of unpleasant consequences if the right action is chosen.

Others, though, choose to commit evil acts in full knowledge of that evil, deliberately. In the Bible, we see David sending Bathsheba's husband Uriah to his death in battle, to cover up an earlier sin (2 Samuel 11:14–15), and Jacob and Rebekah colluding in an elaborate plot to cheat Esau out of his rightful inheritance as the elder son (Genesis 27:5–29).

THE LAW ON OUR HEARTS

We can see, then, that there are many ways in which to choose evil paths, but what might motivate us to make the right choices? Biblically, it appears that good choices in life stem from two main sources: dutiful obedience to God's laws and our own conscience. Conscience is considered far superior to law-keeping as a mature guide to right behaviour.

As the Israelites emerged as a free nation after their slavery in Egypt, God gave them the Ten Commandments (Exodus 20:2–17; Deuteronomy 5:6–21), as well as many other good and necessary laws. These were to be the building blocks of a peaceful, just, ordered society in which the weak and marginalized were guaranteed protection from abuse by more powerful members of the group. By the time of Jesus, however, the Pharisees and other religious leaders had misguidedly piled on top of God's basic commandments layer on layer of other rules and regulations. These rules were designed with the intention of ensuring obedience to God in every detail, but had the effect of weighing down the Israel-ites and obscuring the reasons behind God's laws. So Jesus rebuked the Pharisees: 'woe to you, because you load people down with burdens they can hardly carry, and you yourselves will not lift one finger to help them' (Luke 11:46). Jesus also backed up his rebuke with action, breaking many of the regulations repeatedly and in full view of the Pharisees. For example, he broke rules about 'working' on the Sabbath (Matthew 12:1–13) and ritual washing before meals (Mark 7:1–5).

In fact, Jesus boiled down the whole mass of commandments in the Law of Moses to just two: 'Love the Lord your God with all your heart and with all your soul and with all your mind and with all your strength' and 'Love your neighbour as yourself' (Mark 12:30–31). More than 600 years previously, God had said through the prophet Jeremiah, 'The time is coming... when I will make a new covenant with the house of Israel... I will put my law in their minds and write it on their hearts' (Jeremiah 31:31, 33). He was looking forward to a time when his people would be able to internalize the rules for life that he had given them, so that they would be part of each person's individual conscience rather than being imposed from outside by other people or institutions. This finely tuned conscience, based on an all-encompassing love of God and other people and a mature understanding of the reasons behind the rules rather than a slavish adherence to the letter of the law, is what God looks for in his followers.

We cannot make good choices by mindlessly keeping to a set of rules and regulations. In fact, if we never progress beyond an unthinking attitude of compliance with laws handed down to us from above, we may even lay ourselves open to deception and manipulation by authority figures who would wish to control and enslave us. Instead, we must grasp the law of love that lies behind God's principles and thus write his laws on our heart, our own conscience. In this way, we make full and right use of the free will that God has given us, which, as we have seen, God himself will not undermine or violate. As the writer of Proverbs advised his readers, 'Above all else, guard your heart, for it is the wellspring of life' (Proverbs 4:23).

We are left, however, with the troubling fact that good choices are not easy to make. The gate to life remains 'small' (Matthew 7:14), yet the key to understanding how such choices can be possible lies in the fact that the gate is neither a set of rules nor a pure conscience, but a person. Jesus claimed, 'I am the gate; whoever enters through me will be saved... I have come that they may have life, and have it to the full' (John 10:9, 10). In Christianity, it is primarily our allegiance to the person of Jesus Christ, the small gate personified, that allows us to begin to travel on the narrow road to life. Right choices grow out of a committed relationship with him.

CHOICE OR DETERMINISM IN THE *HARRY POTTER* STORIES?

So what does all this have to do with the *Harry Potter* books? Does the worldview of the books lend support to determinism—that we are moulded helplessly by our genes and our environments—or does it approach a Christian belief in free personal choice between good and evil paths and personal accountability to God?

First of all, it can be said that the *Harry Potter* stories, in common with most secular fiction, make no reference to the idea that we must answer to God for our choices in life. There is also (so far) a very limited emphasis on personal repentance. Therefore, the stories do not include a full-blooded Christian attitude to moral account-ability. Nevertheless, it should be crystal clear, even to a superficial reader of the books, that determinism has no place in them and that the reality of personal choice between good and evil is a foundational theme throughout the story. Of all the 'sub-Christian values' to be found in the books, this is one of the most obvious and significant in the series, including parallels to most of the strands of biblical teaching that I've outlined above.

Harry himself is an independent-minded character whom we see making a brave, deliberate choice for goodness very early on in his encounter with the magical world to which he belongs. In Chapter 6 of *The Philosopher's Stone*, Harry has just struck up a friendship with Ron Weasley on the train journey to Hogwarts School when another boy, Draco Malfoy, comes to their carriage and attempts to advise Harry that the Weasleys are not the right kind of people to mix with and that he, Malfoy, can help Harry not to 'go making friends with the wrong sort' (p. 81). Harry instinctively realizes that Malfoy is a corrupt character and refuses even to shake hands with him, deciding instead to trust his own judgment of Ron's worthiness as a friend. This exchange establishes Harry and Malfoy firmly on opposing 'sides' from the outset, but a far more significant choice awaits Harry on his first evening at school—a choice that needs some careful explanation.

Each student at Hogwarts is placed into one of the four school houses by putting on the 'Sorting Hat'. This thinking, speaking hat decides, on the strength of the student's abilities and personal values, which of the houses is most appropriate for him or her. (In summary, Gryffindors are 'brave at heart', Slytherins are cunning and ambitious, Ravenclaws are intellectual and Hufflepuffs are patient, hardworking and loyal.) Having watched Draco Malfoy being sorted into Slytherin, and knowing that the evil Lord Voldemort was also in Slytherin in his time, Harry takes his turn with the hat, desperately thinking, 'Not Slytherin, not Slytherin.' The hat argues briefly, telling Harry that Slytherin could 'help [him] on his way to greatness', but soon relents and makes a final decision for Gryffindor, placing Harry in a long tradition of great and good wizards, including headmaster Albus Dumbledore himself.

The importance of this incident is not thoroughly explored, however, until *The Chamber of Secrets*, in which Harry discovers that he has a rare ability usually associated with Dark wizards—the ability to talk to snakes. For most of the story, Harry remains seriously worried that the Sorting Hat was right first time—he really 'belongs' in Slytherin—and that he has an evil streak that will eventually gain the upper hand. At last, at the very end of the book, after Harry has overturned Voldemort's latest plan to wreak havoc in the school, he dares to confide his terrible fear to Professor Dumbledore. At this point, Dumbledore leads Harry to understand that he was placed in Gryffindor rather than Slytherin because he made a conscious choice to reject evil, and that this choice is what makes him 'a true Gryffindor'. Probably one of the most 'quotable' lines in *The Chamber of Secrets*, and one that sums up an important theme in the book, is spoken here by Dumbledore: 'It is our choices, Harry, that show what we truly are, far more than our abilities' (p. 245).

This 'sorting' of students on the basis of personal values and potential may seem, at face value, to be a form of determinism: if you're brave, clever or a loyal plodder at the age of 11, you'll do well in life; but if you're already cunning and ambitious at this tender age, you're bound to go wrong as the years roll by. However, the character of Professor Severus Snape proves that this is not necessarily the case. Snape, head of Slytherin house, is an unpleasant, bitter man who harbours a terrible grudge against Harry's dead father and so against Harry himself. However, we discover in *The Goblet of Fire* that Snape was once in the inner circle of Lord Voldemort's followers but renounced Voldemort shortly before the deaths of James and Lily Potter and has been implicitly trusted by Dumbledore ever since. Readers at this point know little else of Snape's history as yet, but we do know that after a childhood of fascination with the 'Dark Arts' he has repented (the only character so far in the series who is known to have done so) and chosen the good side, at the risk of being killed by Voldemort for his betrayal. So, to be sorted into Slytherin does not necessarily mean a lifetime of evil.

TESTING THE QUALITY

In *The Goblet of Fire*, the emphasis on the importance of personal choice between good and evil becomes even clearer than in any of the previous three books. At the climax of the story, Lord Voldemort returns to full power and is once again poised to threaten the wizarding and Muggle worlds with destruction. A furious argument follows between Professor Dumbledore and the Minister for Magic, Cornelius Fudge. Only at this point does the reader understand the significance of the Minister's name, as we hear him 'fudging' the issues surrounding Voldemort's return and trying to pretend that everything can continue as normal. Dumbledore, by contrast, is adamant that measures must be taken to delay Voldemort's progress. It becomes starkly obvious that everyone in the wizarding world—not just people like Harry, on the front line of the battle—is going to have to choose sides and act according to their choice.

With that decision looming on the horizon, we also start to understand that people in the world of the *Harry Potter* stories do not drift into goodness; they are more likely to drift unwittingly into evil unless they make a deliberate decision for good. This, incidentally, is the exact opposite of the view expressed by John Houghton, who, in his book *A Closer Look at Harry Potter*, claims that 'although some of the characters can be clearly identified as going over to the Dark Side, it is assumed that all the rest are by default on the side of light'.[14] The situation at the end of *The Goblet of Fire* leaves no room for any such assumption. Also, the fact that it's all too easy to find oneself on the bad side is reinforced in a speech by Dumbledore that is one of the most moving and memorable in the *Harry Potter* series. In his tribute to Cedric Diggory (a student who became Voldemort's first victim on his return to power), Dumbledore says these words: 'Remember, if the time should come when you have to make a choice *between what is right, and what is easy*, remember... Cedric Diggory' (*GoF*, p. 628, my emphasis). This echoes Jesus' warning about the relative ease of joining the broad path and the difficulty of finding the narrow one

(Matthew 7:14)—and the ability or failure to make that difficult choice will presumably be pivotal to the destinies of the characters in the course of the last books in the series.

There is one person in particular whose destiny is in grave doubt at this critical point in the saga,as the wizarding world stands on the brink of a new war with Voldemort and his followers. Here we see an example of the Proverbs principle that repeated small moral choices add up to good or evil basic character that will either hold firm or be swept away when the storm comes. Percy Weasley, the third Weasley son, has been known since *The Philosopher's Stone* as an ambitious and rather pompous young man. He was overly proud of his position as prefect and then Head Boy at Hogwarts and, in *The Goblet of Fire*, we see how determined he is to work his way up at the Ministry of Magic as quickly as possible (mainly by 'crawling' to his superiors). Throughout all four volumes of the story to this point, Percy has been a figure of fun, teased and ridiculed by his younger brothers in their efforts to take him down a peg or two, but rather indulged by his parents because of his success at school and his generally law-abiding behaviour. Among the multitude of questions that explode in the reader's mind at the very end of *The Goblet of Fire*, however, one of the most intriguing is 'Which side will Percy choose?' Suddenly, pompous Percy isn't so funny any longer. We realize with a shock that, in an effort to protect his own career, he may side with Cornelius Fudge (and, by default, with Voldemort) rather than the rest of his family, who are all, without exception, loyal to Professor Dumbledore. Will Percy be of strong enough character to jump to the right side before it's too late or has his continual nurturing of selfish ambition made him as weak as Fudge himself?

We can clearly see, at this halfway stage in the *Harry Potter* series, that the pressure of Voldemort's return is starting to reveal the quality of each person's character. The sudden crisis reveals Fudge's true nature as someone who is not fully committed to goodness but is instead concerned primarily with protecting his own position of power; Percy is about to show where his true allegiance lies; and we

learn here for the first time that Arthur Weasley's determined
respect and affection for Muggles (non-wizards) has cost him the
chance of promotion at the Ministry over a period of many years
(*GoF*, p. 617). The storm is about to break: who will remain
standing firm when it has swept by (Proverbs 10:25)?

As we read on through *The Order of the Phoenix*, we find that Percy
does indeed put his career first and remains estranged from his
family throughout the book, while the wider magical community
has to choose whether to trust Harry's report of Voldemort's return
or (the more comfortable path) to accept the Ministry of Magic's
stubborn denials.

More importantly, though, in this fifth book, possible flaws begin
to surface in Harry's own character under the pressure of the previous years' trauma—a boiling rage that he seems unable to control,
and an unresolved hatred for Professor Snape (which has been
simmering in him since *The Philosopher's Stone*). The choice between
sides still hangs in the balance for many characters as we approach
the final two books in the series, and even Harry has his work cut
out for him in the fight to control his emotions, channel his anger
in constructive rather than destructive ways and thus prevent
himself from becoming 'easy prey for the Dark Lord' (*OoP*, p. 473).

Dumbledore's reprimand to Cornelius Fudge in *The Goblet of Fire*
carries echoes of yet another biblical principle that we've noted
above—the idea that what matters in life is not the raw material we
start with, but the way in which we invest and develop the gifts we
are given. Fudge is all too ready to stereotype people according to
their origins, whether they are of 'pureblood' wizarding stock or
Muggle parentage, but Dumbledore rebukes him with the words,
'You fail to recognise that it matters not what someone is born, but
what they grow to be!' (*GoF*, pp. 614–615). Once again, this is in
stark contrast with John Houghton's view that there can be 'no
salvation' for Harry's cruel aunt and uncle because 'they are Muggle
born and bred and the rules of birth are everything'.[15] The rules of
moral choice and responsibility must surely apply to Muggles as
well as wizards—they are all human beings—and in the *Harry Potter*

stories the circumstances of one's birth neither determine nor excuse good or bad behaviour.

PATHS INTO EVIL

We've established that the *Harry Potter* books strongly emphasize the need to make a positive choice for goodness, but we also see acted out before us in the stories the full range of ways in which, according to the Anglican Prayer of Confession, people drift into or choose evil paths. Characters who demonstrate negligence, weakness and deliberate fault in their rejection of what is right can all be found in the pages of the *Harry Potter* books.

Draco Malfoy, Harry's worst enemy among his schoolmates, revels in his own nastiness throughout the series. This is never more the case than at the end of *The Goblet of Fire*, when he is rejoicing about the Dark Lord's return. We know by this stage that Draco's sinister father, Lucius, is a 'Death Eater' (a member of Voldemort's inner circle). Draco has therefore had an evil father as a role model for the whole of his life and probably gained the impression from him that to be a follower of Voldemort is to be powerful, with dominance over other supposedly weaker people. He is blind and complacent, therefore, with no respect for goodness and no desire to probe further into the true nature of the evil that lurks in the midst of his family. Draco is not present at the return of Lord Voldemort; he does not witness his father, with the other Death Eaters, cringing and grovelling in fear at the Dark Lord's feet, crawling on their knees to kiss the hem of his robe. It seems likely that if Draco ever came face to face with Voldemort he would be shocked into a realization of the true danger that threatens him in his negligent attitude—but by that time it might be too late to save himself.

By contrast, Peter Pettigrew (also known as Wormtail) is fully aware that Voldemort is an unpleasant person to serve, but he is so weakened by his fear of Voldemort that he is quite unable to break away and do what he knows to be right. Pettigrew, once a close schoolfriend of Harry's father James, is the person who betrayed James and Lily Potter to their deaths at the hands of Voldemort when Harry was 15 months old. In *The Prisoner of Azkaban*, set 12 years after that betrayal, James' other close friends catch up with Pettigrew and challenge him with his horrendous crime. In this scene, Pettigrew is repeatedly confronted with his own cowardice and we realize how this weakness of character, unaddressed since boyhood, has made him impotent in the matter of choosing good paths.

Other people in the story who display particular weaknesses are Professor Gilderoy Lockhart, the Defence Against the Dark Arts teacher in *The Chamber of Secrets*, whose vanity and self-promotion are a cover for his spinelessness and incompetence, and Ginny Weasley, whose innocent use of Voldemort's magic diary (also in *The Chamber of Secrets*), lays her open to ruthless manipulation by him. In Ginny's case, her insecurity, coupled with a sense of isolation that prevents her from confiding even in her own brothers, leads her to commit acts that she herself is revolted by.

Finally, there is at least one character who is fully aware of Voldemort's true nature, shows great strength and determination in carrying out his part in Voldemort's schemes, but commits terrible evil by his own deliberate fault. This character is Barty Crouch Junior. He is the secret villain of *The Goblet of Fire* and succeeds in delivering Harry to the place designated for Voldemort's revival. To the very end, he is proud of his crime, unrepentant and looking forward to being 'honoured' by Voldemort for his part in restoring him to full power.

THE LAW ON HARRY'S HEART

As far as the motivation for making the right choices is concerned, J.K. Rowling treats the subject just as seriously, providing a thought-provoking study of the relative merits of law-keeping and sensitivity to conscience. It is useful here to consider some of the criticisms that have been levelled at Harry by Christians who claim that he makes a habit of disobeying orders and breaking rules, that he is therefore an undesirable role model for children and that the *Harry Potter* books are fundamentally in conflict with a Christian worldview. For example, John Houghton claims that 'Harry Potter, following his own instincts, will break the laws of the Ministry of Magic or the school rules where occasion demands, simply on the grounds of his innate feelings. That kind of autonomy is dangerous. Where everyone does what is right in their own eyes it is the end of civilization and society.'[16] Other Christians have complained that Harry never has to cope with unpleasant consequences for disobedient behaviour and this must encourage readers to expect to get away with disobedience themselves.

Those commentators who believe that the *Harry Potter* stories are based on sound moral foundations, however, argue that rule-keeping, in Christian thought, is not an end in itself and an understanding of the principles behind the rules is vital if we are to develop a mature ability to choose between right and wrong. This idea is discussed in some depth by both Francis Bridger[17] and Connie Neal.[18] To me, the accusation that Harry breaks rules on the grounds of his 'innate feelings', and that this is dangerous, antisocial behaviour, seems to betray a very shallow understanding of the issues involved. In fact, J.K. Rowling explores the question of rule-breaking and obedience in much greater depth than her Christian critics seem to realize.

The magical community is governed by a vast array of laws that are presumably intended to promote a safe, secure society in which wizards and Muggles alike are protected from abuse. There is a Ministry department for the 'Regulation and Control of Magical Creatures' and laws to prevent 'Misuse of Muggle Artefacts', a 'Code of Wand Use' and a 'Decree for the Reasonable Restriction of Underage Sorcery', to name just a few. The wizarding world is by no means anarchic in the way it operates: these laws are seen as a good and necessary aid to just government. On the other hand, it is indeed quite a prominent feature of the story that Rowling's young hero shows, in Dumbledore's words, 'a certain disregard for rules' and usually decides for himself what is the right course of action when faced with a moral dilemma. However, John Houghton's disapproval of the reliance on 'innate feelings' is somewhat puzzling if we bear in mind that another word for these feelings might be 'conscience'. As mentioned earlier, the internalization of ideas about right and wrong is something to which we should aspire if we wish to have God's laws written on our hearts (Jeremiah 31:33).

If we look closely at some of the occasions when Harry breaks rules, it becomes evident that he often acts according to a conscience that leads him to put other people's welfare before his own, even to the point of placing himself in danger. For example, in *The Philosopher's Stone*, Harry disobeys the flying teacher's instruction not to mount his broomstick while she is temporarily absent, but Harry, in doing this, is not disobeying simply for the thrill of it, out of idle rebellion or a desire to show off, but because he is determined to rescue the property of another boy, that has been taken away by Draco Malfoy. Harry's relationship of friendship with Neville Longbottom, and his conviction that Neville's property must be protected from harm, is the motivating force behind his disobedience.

Again, Harry's adventure in the chamber of secrets, where he confronts the memory of Tom Riddle (Voldemort at age 16), is not sanctioned by his teachers—McGonagall notes that he has broken 'a hundred school rules into pieces along the way'—but it is driven entirely by a compassionate desire to rescue Ron's younger sister Ginny from death at the hands of Voldemort. DADA teacher Gilderoy Lockhart refuses to do it, so Harry takes the task on himself. Once again, relationships and the welfare of others take precedence over rules in Harry's conscience.

There is one situation, however, in which Harry might be said to break school rules for deliberately selfish reasons. This is when (in *The Prisoner of Azkaban*) he uses his Invisibility Cloak, Marauder's Map and a secret passageway out of Hogwarts to visit the village of Hogsmeade without the necessary permission slip from his guardians, the Dursleys. However, it should be noted that, unlike the other times mentioned, no good comes of this disobedience for

Harry: it leads to capture and fierce interrogation by Snape and a short but penetrating lecture from Professor Lupin, which brings home to Harry that his desire not to miss out on a treat has put in jeopardy his life and the efficacy of his parents' self-sacrifice on his behalf. It is notable that Lupin's rebuke majors not on the necessity of keeping rules for the sake of keeping rules but on the potentially disastrous consequences of breaking them in this particular case and the need for Harry to honour his relationship to his late parents (*PoA*, p. 213).

This incident, and its fallout for Harry, flies in the face of those critics who say that he never feels any adverse consequences for disobedience. The aftermath of his unauthorized visit to Hogsmeade is a particularly unpleasant experience for Harry. In any case, he is regularly required to serve detention or lose house points as punishment for minor misdemeanours. The justice of such punishments is backed up by Hagrid's comment on one such occasion: 'Yeh've done wrong an' now yeh've got ter pay fer it' (*PS*, p. 182). Harry's detention in this case involves accompanying Hagrid into the terrifying Forbidden Forest to search for an unknown creature that has been killing unicorns there—an experience Harry would have no wish to repeat.

RESISTING TEMPTATION

Most important of all, though, in J.K. Rowling's exploration of rule-breaking is another facet of Harry's reliance on his own conscience as a guide for his behaviour. This is highly significant to the progression of the story, but has been completely overlooked by every anti-Potter commentator I have encountered. The fact is that this independent-minded boy who disregards rules in favour of promoting loving relationships is far less likely than other characters in the story, whether they are his peers or elders, to succumb to the pressure to obey commands from evil people. In *The Goblet of Fire*, we discover that there are three 'Unforgivable Curses' in the wizarding world. They are a killing curse, a torturing curse and a kind of brainwashing curse, called Imperius, which strips away the victim's free will and lays him or her open to emotional, mental and physical manipulation by another person. Harry is found to have an unusual natural ability to resist the Imperius curse so that he can continue to exert his own free will. Mad-Eye Moody, commenting on this resistance, says that it '... takes real strength of character, and not everyone's got it' (GoF, p. 189).

The strength to resist Imperius stands Harry in good stead when he faces the newly revived Voldemort, who arrogantly tells him, '... obedience is a virtue I need to teach you before you die' (GoF, p. 574). Harry is determined that he is not going to obey Voldemort, unlike the circle of Death Eaters who have just been compelled to kneel and kiss the hem of the Dark Lord's robes. As Voldemort attempts to force Harry, under the influence of Imperius, to give him an answer he wants to hear, Harry hears 'a stronger voice, in the back of his head' (his own conscience, we assume) telling him not to reply. Voldemort is naturally infuriated by his failure to manipulate Harry's response, but it is clear that the victory of free will over brainwashing is an important one for Harry and a cause of celebration for the reader of the story.

It seems, therefore, that Harry Potter—much maligned by some Christians for his refusal to obey rules as a matter of course—is actually the one best able to resist temptation when it comes in the form of pressure to obey evil commands. Seen from this angle, the habit of thinking independently and acting according to the dictates of one's conscience, rather than mindlessly following orders, starts to look less like a denial of Christian values and more like an indispensable virtue, vital to living a good life.

PERSONAL RELATIONSHIP

Earlier in this chapter, I mentioned in passing that the members of the Weasley family who are most obviously committed to goodness are all 'loyal to Professor Dumbledore'. This observation is of great importance. Goodness among the wizards we meet in the *Harry Potter* stories is invariably linked with loyalty to Dumbledore. In their own individual strengths and weaknesses, struggles and achievements, J.K. Rowling's fictional characters are no better and no worse than any of us in the real world. However, all the good characters show a fierce allegiance to Dumbledore, and this often stems from a debt of gratitude. (Hagrid and Professor Lupin are two examples of people who owe their position in the school to Dumbledore's intervention on their behalf, a subject that will be explored further in Chapter 3.) There is a pointer here to the fact that Christian virtue grows out of a relationship of love, gratitude and loyalty to the person of Jesus Christ. In the *Harry Potter* books, a similar quality of relationship with Dumbledore—although it does not fundamentally change the nature of the characters—certainly provides strength and encouragement for them to make the difficult moral choices that they face day by day in their personal battles.

IMPLICATIONS FOR TODAY

Many Christians today would bemoan the fact that traditional structures of morality, based on a clear recognition that there are right and wrong choices to be made, are being steadily dismantled in our society. Instead, it is commonplace for people to 'fudge' the issues involved in ethical decision making, becoming blind to the possible consequences of their actions.

With the advent of the *Harry Potter* books, surely there is a sign of hope for us that thousands of people are finding themselves inspired by a story in which courageously choosing what is 'right' rather than what is 'easy' is held up as a precious and costly virtue; a story that highlights many ways to drift unconsciously into the broad paths of evil and shows the destructive consequences of that drift; a story that lays emphasis on the deliberate development of strong character and reliable conscience rather than the victim mentality bred by determinism or the moral weakness that stems from mindless compliance with other people's instructions. These elements are important building blocks on which it is possible to base an understanding of Christian doctrines about the precious nature of our free will, our accountability to God, personal failure to make consistently right choices and, ultimately, the fact that the most vital choice any of us will ever make is whether or not to give our full allegiance to the person of Jesus Christ. This is the choice that really determines our destiny, as it is a choice between life and death that all of us must face.

CHAPTER 3

GRACE, HOPE AND THE
SECOND CHANCE

See, I am doing a new thing! Now it springs up;
do you not perceive it?
ISAIAH 43:19

Dumbledore was the one who stuck up for me... trusts people,
he does. Gives 'em second chances... tha's what sets him apar'
from other Heads, see.
HARRY POTTER AND THE GOBLET OF FIRE, P. 395

A man and a woman stand ashamed and remorseful before God, the terrible realization dawning that there will be no more intimate garden walks with him in the cool of the evening. That relationship of love and joy has been splintered and they are about to be banished from the only home they have known. Life from now on will be marred by toil and pain and will end in death. Yet, in the midst of the divine rebuke comes hope: a deliverer will be born to the human race who will crush the head of Satan and make amends for the sin of Adam and Eve (Genesis 3:15).

Life on earth has become unendurable. Famine, plague and the terrible devastations of war have ripped the heart out of the Earth and its inhabitants, so that they wish only for death. Yet, there is a promise of better things to come: 'a new heaven and a new earth' will be created that will be the ultimate dwelling place of God with us (Revelation 21:1, 3).

Hope, writes the apostle Paul, is one of the three great Christian qualities that will outlast everything else in our experience: 'And now these three remain: faith, hope and love' (1 Corinthians 13:13). As we look at the Bible from beginning to end, it is clear that the story running throughout is one of unquenchable hope. Hope is an element in the very lifeblood of the biblical narrative and, as such, appears in practically every account of God's dealings with his people. It springs up often in the most unexpected places, but it always has to do with the assurance that goodness must prevail over evil and that there is always deliverance to be found in God. Out of the ruination that human beings always manage to leave in their wake, God is able to bring something new and unexpectedly good.

Christian hope is something more than mere wishful thinking. In many cases, our hope for the future is based on specific promises by God, the fulfilment of which we believe to be certain because they are based on blessings that have already been won for us by Christ. We are certain that Satan's power has been totally crushed because Jesus has already taken all the evil that Satan could throw at him on the cross and has emerged alive on the other side of death. Our hope for eternal life within the perfect new creation described in Revelation 21:1 is certain because it is based on the very same events—the death and resurrection of Christ—that have already happened. These grounds for hope are rooted in past events that are still to be fully worked out in present and future experience according to the ongoing promises of God.

However, Christian hope is not necessarily the same as certainty. The first of Paul's top three Christian virtues listed is faith, and Hebrews 11:1 tells us that faith is 'being sure of what we hope for'. This must mean that hope is something less sure than faith. According to *Vine's Expository Dictionary*, the word 'hope' in the New Testament, meaning 'favourable and confident expectation', most often describes simply 'the happy anticipation of good'. By this definition, hope is quite a subjective emotion, but it is no less powerful for that. In fact, I am convinced that this general 'happy anticipation of good' is a vital ingredient in the Christian life and is rooted not in the specific spoken promises of God but in an understanding of certain aspects of his character: he is a God of surprises, who uses infinite creativity in his dealings with us and brings about constantly new, unexpected turns of events.

In Isaiah 64:3, the prophet says, '... when you did awesome things that we did not expect, you came down, and the mountains trembled before you'. Paul, loosely quoting and perhaps reinterpreting the next verse from that passage, says with wonderment, 'No eye has seen, no ear has heard, no mind has conceived what God has prepared for those who love him' (1 Corinthians 2:9). Certainly Paul himself would never have imagined that he would have a personal encounter with Jesus Christ that would turn all his preconceived ideas upside down and propel him into a life of missionary endeavour. Many people can, I'm sure, testify that a commitment to Christ refocused their vision so they could see the surprising plans that God had for their future, new horizons replacing limited expectations. When we're dealing with a God like this, one who not only makes and fulfils good promises but will also spring good surprises on us throughout our lives, no wonder the Christian life can be an adventure story, full of excitement and unexpected twists in the plot. Anything can happen!

THE CHANCE FOR TRANSFORMATION

The fact that God can make these aspects of his character real in our experience is due to his unfathomable grace—the favour he shows to us that is undeserved. That grace is most clearly seen in the forgiveness that Christ won for us by his death on the cross. The free availability of forgiveness enables God to give us second chances in his grace—indeed, to pick us up every time we fall. It's this that motivates us in turn to forgive people who have hurt us, allowing them an unlimited stock of new chances to be reconciled with us. It is a powerful source of hope in life, to know that forgiveness is possible.

Second chances from God come in many guises, tailored to the circumstances of each individual. There is new 'birth' as well as new opportunities for service, even (or especially) for people who had written themselves off or been written off by the rest of society because of their shortcomings or failures. We see this throughout the Bible in the stories of sinful, weak and damaged people being chosen and used in astounding ways by God despite their failings.

A native Hebrew brought up with all the privileges of an Egyptian prince, but handicapped with a speech impediment, blots his copybook severely when he murders a member of his adopted race. Yet, working as a shepherd in the desert, with little prospect of rising to any greater status, Moses is suddenly called by God to lead the people of Israel out of Egypt (Exodus 4:10) on a perilous journey to the promised land. A missionary is needed to take the Christian gospel across land and sea to the Gentiles, so God chooses Paul— a zealous Pharisee with a hatred of the Church and (we suspect) a recurring medical condition that might have fitted him better to staying at home with his books of theology.

Many others are given second chances to fulfil their calling from God after failure. Rebellious Jonah, for example, is rescued from the storm and the belly of a fish to preach salvation to Nineveh, while Peter is gently restored to ministry after his devastating denial of Jesus (John 21:15–17).

It is notable that, in the cases of Moses and Paul especially, God's grace was at work despite their weaknesses. There is no evidence that God alleviated Moses' speech difficulties, and Paul's prayer that his 'thorn in the flesh' be removed met with a definite refusal from God, yet they still made outstanding contributions to the work of God in their time. This happened because of his gracious provision for them.

PURSUIT AND PROTECTION

Another important thing to note is that the grace of God towards us is proactive—it is entirely God's initiative. As Paul wrote to the Romans, 'While we were still sinners, Christ died for us' (Romans 5:8) and Jesus himself said in his story of the woman with the lost coin, in which the woman symbolizes God, 'Does she not light a lamp, sweep the house and search carefully until she finds it?' (Luke 15:8). In the Old Testament, we see God going out of his way to make himself known to people in the depths of despair. Hagar, the lowest of the low in her household, runs away from abuse at the hands of her mistress Sarah, but is found by God in the desert and 'sees' him with gratitude as 'the God who sees me' (Genesis 16:6–13). Similarly, the prophet Elijah flees in panic to the desert to escape Jezebel's murderous threats and collapses in desperation, wishing for death. God pursues him there, however, and speaks to him in an unexpected way—out of silence rather than spectacular events—to restore his faith in God's future plans for him (1 Kings 19).

This principle applies to us, too, hundreds of years after the last words of the Bible were written. God still takes the initiative in searching us out and bringing us back from the places where we wander, lost and unloved, to the place where we belong, in communion with him.

Another demonstration of God's proactive grace is the way he protects and guards his people. The Psalms are full of praise to God for his loving knowledge and protection of us day to day. Psalm 121 is one of the best examples of this, its assertion that the Lord 'watches over us' to keep us from harm being repeated five times. The Bible suggests that in many ways we may be unaware of the full extent of that protection. Psalm 139:5–6 says, 'You hem me in— behind and before; you have laid your hand upon me. Such knowledge is too wonderful for me, too lofty for me to attain.' In 2 Kings 6, we read how Elisha had to pray for his servant's eyes to be opened before the fearful servant realized, on the brink of Israel's battle with the Arameans, that the surrounding hills were full of the protective horses and chariots of God's army.

SHIFTING HORIZONS

The stories of renewed hope in the Bible are numerous, but the three characters mentioned above—Hagar, Elijah and Elisha's unnamed servant—provide pointers to the way in which this hope, inspired by the experience of God's grace, actually works. It is a change of focus—from problem to solution, from old beaten tracks to new horizons, new ways of seeing the circumstances round about, based on the knowledge that God sees, knows and values us.

For people who find themselves bogged down in deep depression, to discover this change of focus can be the first step out of their desperate state. King David was prone to wide swings of emotion, including overwhelming fear and gloom—hardly surprising when we consider the many serious physical dangers that he encountered as a soldier. David, however, finds release from his despair when he deliberately shifts his focus away from the problem that threatens to engulf him and gazes 'upon the beauty of the Lord' (Psalm 27:4), concentrating on his memory of God's past deeds of deliverance (Psalm 22:4–5) and his confidence in the promises of goodness 'stored up' for him in the future (Psalm 31:19).

Other parts of the Bible encourage us to take courage from the experience of those who have gone before us (the 'great cloud of witnesses' of Hebrews 12:1) or to focus our minds on positive thoughts in our fight against weariness or anxiety: '... whatever is noble, whatever is right, whatever is pure, whatever is lovely, whatever is admirable—if anything is excellent or praiseworthy—think about such things' (Philippians 4:8).

The thought of the 'cloud of witnesses' reminds us that our ultimate hope as Christians extends beyond death. Because Jesus has been resurrected to new life, we expect to experience resurrection also. As Paul writes, 'If for this life only we have hoped in

Christ, we are of all people most to be pitied' (1 Corinthians 15:19, NRSV). Our future resurrection, the 'happy anticipation of good' beyond this life, is the hope that puts all our present trials into eternal perspective.

This, then, is the story of the God who, time after time, offers grace, brings hope and gives second chances. He is a God who sees and knows everyone on Earth by name and persistently searches out those who have hardly any idea of his existence. He forgives us, protects us in the midst of danger and constantly speaks and acts to lift our vision, changing our focus from the circumstances and fears that could otherwise overwhelm us to the astonishing, good surprises that he can bring into our experience to keep our relationship with him fresh and adventurous. What is more, all of this starts as a mystery to us: 'no mind has conceived what God has planned for those who love him'.

HOPE BETRAYED

How many non-Christians are aware that this can be the character of the Christian life? How many unbelievers think of the Bible as an adventure story in which God breaks continually into the experience of ordinary people to open up whole new worlds of hope and grace waiting to be discovered? How many people know that the God of Christianity is a God of colourful creativity and mystery? A good proportion of unchurched people today, if they know anything at all about the Bible, think of it as a rule book, with page after page of instructions attempting to tell them in very restrictive terms how they should live their lives—and of the Christian God as a dry, tame, humourless authority figure wheeled out by Christians to rubber-stamp their rules and regulations. In our evangelism and nurturing of new believers, we are less likely to tell enquirers about the uncertainties of the life of faith and more likely to talk about God's faithfulness in keeping his promises.

Postmodern society does not set much store by promises. With the breakdown in family life that we have seen increasingly over the last quarter of the 20th century, many have had their trust betrayed by people—spouses, parents and even children—whose loyalty they might have taken for granted in decades past. To the victims of such betrayal, what meaning does it have to say that God is a father who makes promises to his children?

Neither does postmodern society believe in rules that can be imposed on one person by another simply because that other is in some position of 'authority'. The right of one to instruct another about how he or she should behave is simply not acknowledged.

In postmodern culture, the experience of the current fleeting moment is the only 'reality'. There is nothing to 'learn' from the past and the future may simply never arrive. The myth of human 'progress', so blindly trusted in the dynamic 19th century, when science, technology and medical advances made the future look like a utopia, has been shattered by the realization that our technology has provided us with the means to destroy our whole world several times over and frightening new diseases have taken the place of the old, vanquished killers.

There is perhaps just one element of the life of grace that unbelievers might associate with the Christian religion—forgiveness. Many people know that Christians are meant to forgive those who damage them in some way, but a good proportion of those would say that forgiveness is often an impossible goal. Indeed, it's by no means true that forgiveness is universally acknowledged as a virtue. *The Daily Mail* published an essay by Dr John Casey on 27 June 2001 in which he described acts of forgiveness as 'unmanly and disgusting', and others might agree with him that to forgive one's enemies rather than take revenge is a sign of weakness.

Where is the hope for people in a world like this, with no roots in the past, no trust in the future and nothing stable to hold on to in the present—not even the possibility of forgiveness for wrongs committed and received? It has been said that 'hopelessness is the very definition of postmodernism'.[19] Perhaps it's not surprising, then, that suicide has increased alarmingly over the last three or four decades (by 60 per cent between 1976 and 1991). Suicide is a particular problem among young men, who feel unable to confide their feelings of despair in anyone who might be able to help them. Loss of hope, intensified by a sense of isolation in life, can be a fatal disease. Depressive illness, too, is on the increase among the post-modern generation—the very age group that is abandoning traditional Christianity and the institutionalized Church.

HARRY AND THE HOPE OF DELIVERANCE

J.K. Rowling, it would seem, has an understanding of the fact that, in biblical stories, perceptions can change in an instant, trans-forming gloom to joy and dead ends into new possibilities. In an interview discussion about art, she said, 'Perhaps my favourite painting is Caravaggio's *Supper at Emmaus* when Jesus reveals himself to the disciples having risen from the dead... the painting captures the exact moment when the disciples realize who this man is, blessing their bread.'[20]

Rowling's own stories are driven by repeated instances of joyful transformations (called 'eucatastrophe' by J.R.R. Tolkien in his essay 'On Fairy Tales'), with their unveiling of new horizons, and this is undoubtedly one of the most crucial factors in the success of the *Harry Potter* books. Readers are deeply captivated by the un-predictability of the plot. In Harry's world of adventure and mystery, it seems that anything can happen: the course of events and people's perceptions of their own and others' circumstances can be changed in the blink of an eye. It is clear that at the root of the reader's fascination with the twists and turns of the story is a 'happy anticipation of good'—the all-pervading sense that, however difficult things may be for Harry and his friends, hope is bubbling close to the surface and deliverance is ultimately certain.

This fire of unquenchable hope is ignited at the very beginning of *The Philosopher's Stone*, when the wizarding world receives its first inkling that Lord Voldemort has been shockingly defeated by the most unlikely person—a seemingly defenceless baby boy, the son of James and Lily Potter.

To understand this, it is important to enter emotionally into the full impact of Harry's survival of Voldemort's attack. The evil wizard has held the magical community in the grip of terror and despair for a number of years before the start of the first book in the series— killing indiscriminately, torturing others to the point of insanity and controlling the minds and behaviour of many so that it is impossible to tell who are his true followers and who are those who have simply become victims of brainwashing. The fear of Voldemort is so great that very few wizards dare even speak his name. Then, suddenly, completely without warning or explanation, a 15-month-old baby boy survives an attack that should have been fatal, as so many previous attacks have proved to be. The evil one goes into hiding, his power shattered, and freedom returns to the wizarding world, all because of the inexplicable escape of 'Harry Potter—the boy who lived!'

Many well-known fantasy writings include specific prophecies that serve to focus hope on the major characters in the story. In the *Star Wars* saga, there is a prophecy of a great Jedi Knight who will 'bring balance to the Force'—a hope that is dashed when the promised one, Anakin Skywalker, turns to the Dark Side and becomes Darth Vader. In C.S. Lewis' *The Lion, the Witch and the Wardrobe*, the coming of two sons of Adam and daughters of Eve to sit on the four thrones at Cair Paravel is foretold,[21] while in Tolkien's *The Lord of the Rings*, a rhyme foretells the return of a king who has many names, one of which, Estel, actually means 'hope'.[22]

In common with these other examples of the genre, J.K. Rowling's fantasy contains just such a prophecy, although it is not revealed until the end of *The Order of the Phoenix*. Throughout the first four volumes of the story, the vital question of why Lord Voldemort set out to kill baby Harry in the first place remained unanswered (inspiring much wild speculation among Potter fans). We now know, however, that Harry is indeed a promised deliverer— marked as 'the one with the power to vanquish the Dark Lord'

(*OoP*, p. 741). The prophecy does not guarantee that Harry *will* finally vanquish Voldemort, only that he will have the *power* to do it, so in that sense it does not provide a sure hope of deliverance.

Nevertheless, Harry's fellow wizards do not need to hear the prophecy to have a 'confident expectation' that he will overcome the Dark Lord. The fact that, as a baby, he has already unexpectedly stripped Voldemort of his evil power and cheated death at Voldemort's hands makes him a powerful sign of hope at the very outset of the story. More to the point, the scar on his forehead, which is the telltale mark of his escape from death—the thing that identifies him beyond doubt as the potential vanquisher of the Dark Lord—becomes a legend within the wizarding world. Everyone who is introduced to Harry by name instinctively glances up to his forehead to check out the scar and anyone who first notices the scar under Harry's hair immediately realizes that they are face to face with one of the most famous wizards alive.

Among her fascinating essays on the Seven Deadly Sins and Seven Heavenly Virtues in the *Harry Potter* stories, Peg Kerr points out that there is a paradox at the beginning of *The Philosopher's Stone*: 'while Harry is the embodiment of hope for the wizarding world, he has absolutely no hope for himself'.[23] Instead, Harry is exiled from the world he has saved and lives for the next ten years as the virtual prisoner of his aunt and uncle, the Dursleys. Yet, the time for hope to be restored to Harry himself does come.

HARRY PURSUED AND PROTECTED

We've noted that God's grace is proactive in our lives in the way that he pursues those he calls, even to the point where we are at the end of ourselves, and in the way that he protects us, often without our knowledge. In the *Harry Potter* stories, both of these signs of grace are pictured in Harry's own experience. At the end of his ten years' exile and imprisonment, Harry's first inkling that representatives from a strange new world are trying to reach him is when a letter arrives for him at his aunt and uncle's house, addressed personally to 'Mr H. Potter, The Cupboard under the Stairs, 4 Privet Drive, Little Whinging, Surrey'. Uncle Vernon intercepts and reads the letter, realizes that it's from Hogwarts and destroys it, feeling horrified and shamed by the pinpoint accuracy of the address. Someone—like the God who 'saw' Hagar on her knees in the desert (Genesis 16:13)—knows Harry by name and knows exactly where to find him. What follows, as 4 Privet Drive is flooded with letters over the next few days, is a frantic attempt by Uncle Vernon to outwit the mysterious letter writer and prevent any further contact.

Mr Dursley's final act of evasion is to take the family across the sea to a rundown shack on an island, where Harry spends the night before his eleventh birthday trying to sleep on the bare floor of the hovel. At last, on the stroke of midnight, Rubeus Hagrid, Keeper of Keys and Grounds at Hogwarts School, breaks down the door and introduces himself as an emissary for Albus Dumbledore, come to ensure that Harry receives his invitation to Hogwarts in person. A little later in the chapter comes, for me, one of the most moving sentences in the series: 'Harry stretched out his hand at last to take the yellowish envelope, addressed... to Mr H. Potter, The Floor, Hut-on-the-Rock, The Sea' (*PS*, p. 42). An 11-year-old boy, un-loved, unwanted, abused, has been relentlessly pursued and found, on the floor of an isolated shack, by someone who knows, values and cares about him as a very special individual—someone who is absolutely determined to rescue him from despair and bring him to the place where he truly belongs.

Later in the story, we learn that throughout Harry's young life since Voldemort's failed attack, Professor Dumbledore has made himself responsible for Harry's protection. We discover that Harry has been 'protected in ways that he knows nothing about'. Of course, because the story is written almost entirely from Harry's point of view, if Harry is ignorant of something, so are we readers. However, one strand of that secret protection is revealed in *The Goblet of Fire* for those readers who keep their eyes open. It is heavily hinted there that the neighbour who used to look after the young

Harry whenever his aunt and uncle went away without him, Mrs Figg, is not in fact a Muggle. The fifth book confirms that Arabella Figg is a member of the Order of the Phoenix, charged by Dumbledore with the responsibility of keeping an eye on Harry through his childhood in Little Whinging. The sudden awareness that this nondescript, rather unappealing old woman, whose house always stank of cats and overcooked cabbage, has actually been a watchful but unrecognized guardian over Harry for years is a joyful surprise to the reader—perhaps not as shocking a revelation as Elisha's servant received when God opened his eyes to see the armies of the Lord (2 Kings 6:17), but a revelation nonetheless of one way in which Dumbledore has been protecting Harry, without his knowledge, from his earliest days.

HARRY'S NEW HORIZONS

In common with most adventure stories in which the hero invariably escapes from 'certain death' at the last possible moment, Harry's later encounters with evil bring him often to the brink of despair, only to be rescued into new hope by completely unforeseen means. In some of these situations, it is clear that Harry's escape comes when he shifts his focus from the danger that threatens him to some other source of goodness, either within or outside himself.

In *The Prisoner of Azkaban*, we see Harry saved from a fate worse than death by his determination to concentrate on goodness rather than evil. The Dementors—the grey, blind, hooded guards of Azkaban wizards' prison who are introduced in this third book of the series—are, according to J.K. Rowling herself, consciously intended to be representations of depression.[24] They literally suck happiness, hope and all positive emotion from the air around them wherever they go, and their final weapon is to suck the very soul from their victims.

What remedy is there in the *Harry Potter* stories against these personifications of depression and despair? For Harry himself, the battle is discovered to be particularly gruelling, because the Dementors' effect on him is especially severe. When the first of these ghastly creatures comes near him, Harry starts to hear the voice of his mother, screaming for mercy from Voldemort in her final moments, and he passes out, overcome by the sense of drowning in a sea of icy cold. The emotional experience was described in reality by King David thousands of years ago: 'My heart is in anguish within me; the terrors of death assail me. Fear and trembling have beset me; horror has overwhelmed me' (Psalm 55:4–5). Professor Lupin offers to teach Harry some 'very advanced magic' to combat these distressing effects. This magic is the Patronus charm, which, if performed successfully, causes a silvery guardian to erupt from the wizard's wand and drive the Dementors away. The ability to produce the silver Patronus depends on the wizard's ability to force his focus away from the drowning sensation and concentrate instead on a happy memory or an inspiring promise of hope for the future.

In Harry's case, when he finally produces a Patronus in the moment of his direst need in *The Prisoner of Azkaban*—as a Dementor is closing in on him to rob him of his soul—his Patronus takes the form of a stag, which in turn represents Harry's late father, James. Nothing but the thought of his father is found to be adequate protection for Harry against depression and despair. His hope of rescue is the inspiration he draws from his belief in his father's goodness, love and nobility. 'Whatever is noble... admirable... excellent or praiseworthy—think about such things', says the apostle Paul (Philippians 4:8). Such thoughts serve as our 'Patronus' in reality.

DUMBLEDORE'S GRACE

Just as the characters' choice between good and evil is linked firmly with their attitude to Professor Dumbledore, their experience of hope and grace also often stems from the influence of that one person. It is Dumbledore who arranges for Harry's childhood protection; it is Dumbledore who sends Hagrid to find Harry in the Hut-on-the-Rock; it is the thought of Dumbledore that gives Harry peace and renewed courage in his encounter with Voldemort at full strength. Perhaps it should not be surprising, then, that in the *Harry Potter* stories, Albus Dumbledore is also known as a person who willingly gives second chances to people others would write off and cast aside without a second thought. At least three people in the story so far owe their present situation to this gracious characteristic of the Headmaster. As I mentioned in the previous chapter, Professor Snape changed sides in the battle between good and evil at some time before the story begins—he changed from being a supporter of Lord Voldemort to being loyal to Dumbledore. Harry, Ron and Hermione find it terribly difficult to believe that Snape really is a good guy and, on more than one occasion, Harry asks Professor Dumbledore why he is so sure that Snape can be trusted. Dumbledore invariably declines to tell Harry his reasons: 'That, Harry, is a matter between Professor Snape and myself' (*GoF*, p. 524). As readers, we too have to trust Dumbledore's judgment and give Snape the benefit of the doubt.

Rubeus Hagrid, groundskeeper at Hogwarts, is the second person whose position at the school is dependent on Dumbledore's grace. There are two things about Hagrid that would, to a less enlightened Headmaster, make him a candidate for immediate dismissal. First, Hagrid was expelled from Hogwarts in his third year as a student, but for a misdemeanour that he did not commit. At the time, Dumbledore (then Transfiguration teacher at the school) was the only person who believed in Hagrid's innocence, and he was the one who made sure that Hagrid did not have to leave the school entirely but was offered the position of Keeper of Keys and Grounds. For this reason, Hagrid is fiercely loyal to Dumbledore and will not hear a word said against him. Second, Hagrid has a secret that is revealed only in *The Goblet of Fire*: his mother was a giantess—and giants are hated and feared in the wizarding world. (Ron's humorously lame explanation of this prejudice is, 'Well, they're...

they're... not very nice', *GoF*, p. 374.) When the secret is splashed over the front page of the *Daily Prophet* by nasty journalist Rita Skeeter, Hagrid's confidence takes a nose-dive, but it is Dumbledore (along with Harry, Ron and Hermione) who lifts him out of the pit and encourages him to hold his head high in the school.

The third beneficiary of Dumbledore's determination to give chances to disadvantaged people is Professor Remus Lupin. Lupin also has a dark secret that has made him, in J.K. Rowling's own words, a 'damaged person'. He has been a werewolf since childhood, an outcast from society, poverty-stricken, shabby and prematurely ageing. We learn in *The Prisoner of Azkaban* (in which Lupin takes up the post of Defence Against the Dark Arts teacher) that Dumbledore was the one who made special provision for Lupin to attend Hogwarts School from the age of 11 and also to become a teacher at the school, against the advice of most other staff members, most notably Severus Snape (who ought to know better, given his own situation).

Professor Snape, Hagrid and Professor Lupin are all recipients of grace, all benefiting from Dumbledore's determination to 'give people chances'. None of these characters is completely trans-formed by the chances they are given: Snape is still a bitter man; Hagrid cannot change his ancestry and remove the stigma of giants' blood or, indeed, the stigma of expulsion from school 50 years ago; Lupin is still a werewolf, dependent on a potion to be drunk every full moon to keep him from attacking others. In their own unique weakness, however, each one is provided with the resources they need to make a valuable contribution to Hogwarts School, under the watchful care of Headmaster Dumbledore.

THE GRACE OF FORGIVENESS

As I've mentioned, in terms of Christian experience, forgiveness is a consequence of the grace of God and a powerful source of hope in life. Forgiveness is what precipitates second chances (indeed, in the teaching of Jesus, there is a never-ending stream of new chances). Does this important virtue figure at all in the *Harry Potter* series? Not according to one critic, Karen Jo Gounaud of the US 'Family Friendly Libraries', who complains that the stories emphasize 'revenge and dominance rather than reconciliation, forgiveness, and serving others'.[25]

This is an extraordinary claim to make, given the events of *The Prisoner of Azkaban*. In this book, Ron and Hermione fall out with each other over the behaviour of their respective pets (Hermione's cat appears to have eaten Ron's rat). Two chapters later, there is mutual forgiveness, a reconciliation takes place and the pair work together to serve their mutual friend, Hagrid. In *The Goblet of Fire*, it's Harry and Ron who fall out, and Hermione does everything possible to reconcile them. The pain suffered by the trio during the three weeks when Harry is bereft of his closest companion is palpable to the reader, and when the boys do bury the hatchet, Hermione cries tears of joy. In these incidents, the three friends' partnership is severely tested, but forgiveness wins through and leaves the bonds between them stronger than ever before.

HOPE BEYOND DEATH

Dumbledore's assertion to Harry, in *The Philosopher's Stone*, that 'death is but the next great adventure' (p. 215) provides the smallest of hints that death may not be the end for human beings in Harry's world, but the next three books in the series are silent on the matter. After the death of Cedric Diggory, Dumbledore can only say, with a heavy heart, 'No spell can reawaken the dead' (*GoF*, p. 605). In other words, nothing in the wizards' armoury of magic can provide any hope of resurrection, and premature death is portrayed as something agonizing, puzzling and utterly devastating to those who are left behind (as it is in real life also).

The death of his godfather, Sirius Black, is another terrible blow to Harry, made doubly unbearable as his hopes of ever seeing or speaking to Sirius again are dashed. Yet Harry has heard the murmur of voices behind the strange, fluttering veil hanging from an archway in the Ministry Department of Mysteries—and Luna Lovegood's calm assurance that her own dead mother is among those 'just lurking out of sight' there leaves him with the realization that 'the terrible weight in his stomach seemed to have lessened slightly' (*OoP*, p. 761).

Nothing in our real life or any author's fantasy comes close to the certain hope expressed in the Christian doctrine of the resurrection of the dead, but here in the *Harry Potter* story is the promise that death is not the end—that although contact between the two sides of the veil is impossible, there is life to be found beyond it.

IMPLICATIONS FOR TODAY

In the *Harry Potter* books we see the grace of forgiveness portrayed; we witness second chances being given to weak, sinful and damaged people; we see the proactive protection, pursuit and rescue of an exiled, desperate young boy; and we watch in amazement as hope springs from undreamed-of sources, lifting vision and shifting focus from the experience of overwhelming horror to a way of escape.

The fact that millions of people worldwide, young and old, male and female, are riveted by this saga must show that human beings have an insatiable hunger to experience hope and grace, a hunger that springs from an inbuilt knowledge that evil cannot last forever and must ultimately be defeated by goodness. We may live in a real world that sometimes seems hopeless, depressing and full of overwhelming gloom, but stories like those in the *Harry Potter* books grab the imagination and turn it outwards to grasp the vision of change for the better.

There are many readers of these books who have no knowledge at all of the Christian God who is the source of real-life hope, grace and second chances. Yet these readers know very well that these things exist in Harry's world and would love to see them demonstrated in their own life's story. Perhaps it is time for Christians to shake the dust off the 'rule book' that the Bible appears to be for many unbelievers, and start to reveal the God of creativity, mystery, surprises and adventure who has been locked inside it for too long, the God who does 'awesome things that we do not expect'. This is not to paint a rosy picture of a Christian life without commitments, difficulties or hardships. The message from the *Harry Potter* stories is that hope may rise in the midst of danger, and grace may be extended in the midst of weakness and inability. The same is true in the biblical story and in the testimony of many of us contemporary Christians.

In a hopeless world, the minds of *Harry Potter* fans are primed to receive the news that goodness can and does overcome the worst that evil can throw at us in this life. Can we grasp the opportunity to let them know that this can be true in reality, in a real experience of God, not just in fantasy novels?

Furthermore, the latest episode in J.K. Rowling's story has begun to examine the destructiveness of death more closely than ever, and this may mean that readers begin to face questions about mortality more seriously themselves. Harry's tragic losses reveal a void that only Christianity can truly fill—the finality of death, answered by the prospect of resurrection and eternal life in a world purged of every form of evil. Is the Church communicating this hope to Harry's fans?

CHAPTER 4

THE TRIUMPH OF GOODNESS

*And having disarmed the powers and authorities, he made a public
spectacle of them, triumphing over them by the cross.*
COLOSSIANS 2:15

So. Your mother died to save you. Yes, that's a powerful counter-charm.
HARRY POTTER AND THE CHAMBER OF SECRETS, P. 233

If the Bible provides stories of hope triumphing over despair, it also
gives us stories of goodness triumphing over evil. Hope, as we've
seen, is 'the happy expectation of good'. If hope is victorious, evil
must, by definition, be on its way to defeat.

How exactly does good defeat evil in the Bible? As Christians, we
might tend to think that there is an easy, obvious answer to this
question. In fact, there is a combination of factors at work—some
more important than others but all interrelated with each other.

LOVE AND SELF-SACRIFICE

Let's start with the 'obvious' answer. The central doctrine of the
Christian faith is that the willing, self-sacrificial death of Jesus Christ
on the cross destroyed the power of Satan and sent him reeling in
confusion and terror, releasing every human being in the world,
as well as the created universe itself, from the power of his evil

dominion. A great deal of theological study has gone into explaining the mechanics of Christ's victory. For example, we can imagine it in terms of the cancellation of an unpayable debt (Colossians 2:14) or an exchange of Christ's purity for our wickedness (Isaiah 53:4–5). The full implications of the act are, however, I am sure, far beyond our comprehension. How God, the creator and sustainer of the universe, could give up his own life to win back his creation from the devil's control is an inexplicable mystery.

Even the motivation for Jesus' self-sacrifice might be hard for us to grasp. It was simply that he loved us (John 3:16; Ephesians 5:2). Love is, of course, the very definition of God himself (1 John 4:8, 16) and the quality on which the whole of the Old Testament Law and Prophets hang (Matthew 22:40). Paul's famous words in 1 Corinthians 13 mark out love as the greatest of the enduring Christian virtues, while Song of Songs—the only book of the Bible devoted entirely to the celebration of human passion—includes the beautiful assurance that 'love is as strong as death, its jealousy unyielding as the grave. It burns like blazing fire, like a mighty flame. Many waters cannot quench love; rivers cannot wash it away' (Song of Songs 8:6–7a). Completely selfless love, giving without expecting any payback, is another aspect of the mystery.

If it is difficult for us, people made in God's image, to comprehend 'how wide and long and high and deep is the love of Christ' (Ephesians 3:18), how much harder must it be for Satan himself, devoid of any such quality? C.S. Lewis imagines his senior devil, Screwtape, agonizing over God's love for his creation: 'All His talk about Love must be a disguise for something else—He must have some *real* motive for creating them and taking so much trouble over them... What does He stand to make out of them? That is the insoluble question.'[26]

Perhaps this incomprehension is the reason why Satan was so badly fooled as to think that he would be the victor when Christ died. Although the Bible does not say so explicitly, one way of reading the accounts in the Gospels is that Jesus' execution was the work of Satan, not of God, so Satan must have thought that this would be to his own advantage. Luke 22:3 records that 'Satan entered Judas, called Iscariot', motivating him to agree to betray Jesus, while the group of religious leaders who had long been plotting Jesus' demise are described by Jesus as children of the devil, deceitful and murderous (John 8:44). Allowing himself to believe that he was at last a step ahead of Almighty God, the idea of resurrection from the dead simply never entered Satan's thoughts. Neither did he conceive of the fact that Jesus knew exactly what was happening and was actually moving purposefully towards an act of willing self-sacrifice. As Job 28:22 suggests, God may conceal his wisdom so cleverly that 'Destruction and Death say, "Only a rumour of it has reached our ears."' Satan's ignorance contributed significantly to his downfall: the worst atrocity that he could conceive— the murder of God himself—was recognized too late as the one act that could achieve the redemption of the whole created order.

Here, in a nutshell, I have drawn a picture of the good–evil conflict on a cosmic, heavenly scale, in which Christ spiritually 'disarmed the powers and authorities... triumphing over them by the cross' (Colossians 2:15). Paul insists that even when we confront evil people in the physical world of our everyday lives, a spiritual battle is in progress: 'For our struggle is not against flesh and blood, but against the rulers, against the authorities, against the powers of this dark world and against the spiritual forces of evil in the heavenly realms' (Ephesians 6:12).

STRENGTH IN WEAKNESS

The notion of the battle between good and evil being based in the spiritual world, fought between the ruling powers of the heavenly realm, is by and large a New Testament idea. In the Old Testament, the conflict is a very much a physical, earthbound affair, with 'goodness' seeming to be personified by the Israelites, the chosen people of God, and 'evil' by the surrounding nations—the Egyptians, Philistines and Midianites, for example. When we read Old

Testament stories of victory for the Israelite army and the massacre of thousands of their enemies, we might feel that these accounts contradict the New Testament idea of a battle against spiritual powers rather than flesh and blood.

Nevertheless, there are hints in the Old Testament that spiritual principles are at work in the conflict, even if the battles are fought between very human beings with physically devastating results. For example, we learn that personal weakness and disadvantage may be powerful when submitted to God, and that strength may be found in people and armies of small size but great faith and courage. So Moses and the dispossessed Israelite slaves escape the might and fury of Egypt, on foot, opposed by an army of horses and chariots (Exodus 14); Gideon is commanded to reduce the size of his army to a ridiculous level before engaging the Midianites in battle (Judges 7); and the boy David defeats the Philistine giant Goliath without defensive armour and with a single well-aimed stone (1 Samuel 17).

The Old Testament also affirms, perhaps more clearly than the New, that evil is ultimately self-destructive—corrupting and destroying those who serve it. 'The evil deeds of a wicked man ensnare him; the cords of his sin hold him fast. He will die for lack of discipline, led astray by his own great folly,' says Proverbs 5:22–23. Also, Proverbs 1:32 warns those who reject God that 'the waywardness of the simple will kill them, and the complacency of fools will destroy them'.

THE COSMIC BATTLE DAY TO DAY

So, the two very different periods before and after the coming of Christ both offer important insights about the nature of the battle between good and evil. To us, living 2000 years into the New Testament era, it's obvious that our world is still suffering from the effects of evil, even though Satan has received a devastating blow. Paul's words quoted above, from Ephesians 6, remind us that the struggle against evil continues to this day—and the very fact that

Paul felt it necessary to instruct the Ephesians in this way shows that it is easy to make the mistake of thinking that we are in a conflict with flesh and blood. In our everyday lives, spiritual goodness and evil clothe themselves in human relationships at every level, whether between national and international leaders and the people they serve (or dominate) or between friends, neighbours, business colleagues or fellow road users. The cosmic victory of Christ is of benefit to us only after death unless it is played out in those sometimes humdrum relationships. As Christians, we believe that Jesus is not only our spiritual Saviour, he is also the model for our behaviour—our aim should be to grow more Christ-like and thus overcome evil with good in our earthly lives, day to day. This means that we need to take careful note of Jesus' teaching on how to respond to those who behave wickedly in the world.

MERCY AND SERVICE

In his Sermon on the Mount, Jesus took the great spiritual principles of love and self-sacrifice and applied them to the individual relationships that are the stuff of human life, teaching that the way to defeat evil within those relationships is to act mercifully, without aggression. So, whereas in the Old Testament God commanded his people to take revenge up to the point of equal damage but not beyond ('Show no pity: life for life, eye for eye, tooth for tooth, hand for hand, foot for foot', Deuteronomy 19:21), this standard is no longer acceptable for those living under the new covenant. Instead, we are to accept rough, unjust treatment from evil people and even invite them to give us more of the same (Matthew 5:38–41; Luke 6:29–30). We are told to love our personal enemies and 'be merciful' (Luke 6:35, 36) rather than seek retribution for wrongs. Paul explains that, in so doing, we 'heap burning coals' on the heads of the evildoers, shaming them in the eyes of onlookers (Romans 12:20; quoting Proverbs 25:22).

Another important principle that Jesus taught and modelled was to associate freely with people of low social status and reputation, making no distinctions of class, gender or ethnic background and aiming primarily to serve other people (Mark 2:15; Luke 22:25–26; John 4:9, 27). This is a powerful antidote to the evils of pride, snobbery and selfish ambition that are plain to see in most human organizations, where people tread each other down to satisfy their craving for approval and recognition (Luke 20:46–47; John 7:3–10). Anyone who has worked for long in an environment where there is a sharply defined management structure will know about this syndrome. It is seen also in the wickedness of racist political systems where genetic or cultural differences determine one's supposed human worth.

COURAGE, MUTUAL HELP AND UNITY

For those of us with a Christian background, these teachings of Jesus are so familiar that we can remain blind to the fact that the daily fight against evil people and systems, if we take it seriously, is difficult, tiring, painful and dangerous. Jesus himself was executed because his radical goodness was unbearable to the religious leaders of his time and culture. Many of the early Christians were martyred because they maintained their integrity in the face of blasphemous secular authorities. Truly Christ-like goodness is an offence to the religious and the godless alike and will inevitably lead to opposition from one or the other group, or even both at once.

This means that if we are to confront the wrongs in our world, we need to exercise courage. Without it, our eternal salvation may be secure but we will never make a real difference in the everyday struggle between good and evil. There are some Christians who suggest that because Christ has won the ultimate victory against sin and death, we may sit back and bask in the glory, confident that all will be well in the end. This is an inadequate response. Neither is it acceptable for us to quote the scriptural principle that God's power is made perfect in our weakness (2 Corinthians 12:9) or that 'God

chose the weak things of the world to shame the strong' (1 Corinthians 1:27) to mask our fear or complacency. As the 18th-
century politician Edmund Burke is believed to have said, 'The only
thing necessary for the triumph of evil is for good men to do
nothing.'

Every biblical hero or heroine, whether of the Old or New
Testament, had to gather up their natural gifts and abilities, along
with sheer courage, and put them to use, trusting that God would
meet them halfway and provide the power for full victory. Thus
David used his long-practised skill with sling and stone, added his
personal boldness and faith in God and so succeeded in felling
Goliath against the odds. Moses did as God asked and courageously
stepped out into the barren desert with frightened Israelites in tow.
Also, the Red Sea did not part entirely of its own accord: Moses had
to raise his staff over the sea before seeing the miracle happen
(Exodus 14:16, 21). Paul used both his formidable intellect and his
practical ability in tent-making in his work, braving tempestuous
seas and hostile crowds to preach about the crucified Christ.

Furthermore, in order to be successful in battling evil, we need
the help both of God and of other people. The writer to the
Hebrews encourages his readers to 'consider how we may spur one
another on towards love and good deeds' and reminds them of
times when, in the face of suffering, they 'stood side by side' with
those of their number who were persecuted (Hebrews 10:24,
32–33). David also relied on the loyal friendship of Jonathan
to enable him to escape from the murderous jealousy of Saul
(1 Samuel 20). Jesus himself had a team of indispensable close
friends, though he would have dearly loved to have had their
support in the garden of Gethsemane as he fought his most
gruelling battle with Satan (Mark 14:32–40).

In the Church, unity between believers is a vital component in
the fight against evil. Jesus' prayer for his disciples just before his
death included the request 'that they may be one' (John 17:11),
and the importance of unity is often stressed in the letters of Paul.
For example, he makes a point of pleading with two members of

the Philippian church, Euodia and Syntyche, 'to agree with each other in the Lord' (Philippians 4:2), and urges the whole church in Ephesus to 'make every effort to keep the unity of the Spirit through the bond of peace' (Ephesians 4:3). Ephesians 4:31 instructs the believers further: 'Get rid of all bitterness, rage and anger, brawling and slander, along with every form of malice.' Paul allows that anger against other people may not, in itself, be a sin, but he warns the Ephesians not to allow their anger to fester, as this would 'give the devil a foothold' in their church (Ephesians 4:27).

So we can see that Jesus' death on the cross, while absolutely foundational to a Christian understanding of the triumph of goodness, is also like a huge pebble sending ripples across the lake of the whole of human experience. Selfless love, along with the willingness to sacrifice our lives for others and act mercifully towards our enemies, are qualities that we must bring down to earth if we, in partnership with God, are to make a dent in the evil systems of our world. They must be applied courageously, in the knowledge that small, seemingly insignificant actions can have great effects—and we must be open to receiving support, both human and divine, as we take our stand.

Finally, and perhaps most important of all, we must recognize that the battle between good and evil is most ferociously fought within ourselves. Jesus said that 'from within, from the human heart' comes all manner of evil (Mark 7:21–22, NRSV), and Paul was uncompromising in his assertion that we need to 'take captive every thought to make it obedient to Christ' (2 Corinthians 10:5). This brings us back again to the death of Christ, which takes full effect in each of us only as we admit the evil that lurks in our own hearts.

NO RADICAL GOODNESS

As Christians, we may think that the self-sacrificial death of Christ is the obvious answer to the question of how good conquers evil in reality. However, at Easter 2000 *The Sun* reported the findings of a Gallup poll. The poll found that nearly half of the people in Britain do not know that the death of Christ is commemorated on Good Friday. Indeed, as belief in absolute values ebbs away with the advance of postmodernism, the very idea that goodness and evil might be distinct from and opposed to one another could be disappearing from our national consciousness. The word 'evil' is applied to crimes that are still rightly considered particularly heinous in our society, such as terrorist attacks on innocent people or the sexual abuse of children, but we seldom hear the opinion voiced that evil resides in every individual heart, in the petty quarrels, the power-seeking and exploitation of others that occur daily in the families and businesses that make up the fabric of our lives. Perhaps this is because we do not see much radical goodness demonstrated—even by the Church, which claims to be its advocate. Without that radical goodness, there is nothing with which to compare the prevailing view that, as long as one does no real harm, one is a good enough person, and nothing to counter the idea that whatever 'feels right to me' in a given situation is an acceptable course of action.

There are, from time to time, but rarely, notable exceptions to this norm—when particular evils are confronted and conquered or, at least, reined in for a time. Jesus' teaching about non-retaliation towards enemies might seem simply ridiculous to many non-Christians—and like an impossible ideal to many Christians—but Revd Martin Luther King Jr put it into practice in the 1960s and succeeded in laying the foundation for Black civil rights in the USA. When a victory like this happens, it is usually because one person has the courage and vision to stand up, come out of hiding and use whatever small tools are at hand to oppose the forces arrayed against them.

Another such person in fairly recent history has been Bob Geldof KMG, who in 1984 mounted a campaign to raise money for famine relief in Ethiopia. Geldof's first reaction on seeing the TV pictures of dying children was to think:

What could I do? I could send some money... But that was not enough. To expiate yourself truly of any complicity in this evil meant you had to give something of yourself... I was only a pop singer. And by now not a very successful pop singer... All I could do was make records...[27]

In the subsequent making of the Christmas charity record 'Do They Know It's Christmas?' Geldof was met by more-than-willing co-operation from fellow musicians, and by a series of remarkable 'coincidences':

It is not normal for Sting, for example, to even be in the country, but to find him at home in the afternoon when I rang was extraordinary. It happened not once but often... doors impenetrable a week earlier swung open effortlessly. I thought it was something to do with the fact that I wasn't doing it for myself.[28]

Bob Geldof claims no Christian commitment, yet he fought widespread starvation with an attitude of love and self-sacrifice, combined with bravery, help from friends and, I believe, help from God himself. These are the ingredients for the triumph of goodness over evil.

GOODNESS MUST PREVAIL

As I have said, this kind of victory is rarely seen in real life, but the appetite among millions of people for fantasy stories in which good conquers bad is as strong as ever. In many such stories, the good guy appears to win the fight as a result of having superior strength, intelligence and/or firepower. The *James Bond* movies are a classic example of this approach. There are some stories, however, that illustrate a different philosophy. In the *Star Wars* films, for example, there is a most unusual recognition that the battle against evil has to take place within the hero's own heart, not just against bad people 'out there' somewhere. The moment at the end of *The Return of the Jedi* when Luke Skywalker throws aside his weapon and refuses to kill Darth Vader, because he knows that if he does so he himself will fall to the 'Dark Side of the Force', was a quite new departure in good-versus-evil fantasy sagas.

Everyone who enjoys reading fantasy literature of this type, in which there is a struggle between good and evil, hopes and expects that good will prevail. Everyone knows, at a deep level (which surely reflects the image of God in us), that the story cannot and will not end while evil has the upper hand. In this, we show a deep human instinct to fight on to rescue, heal and restore justice.

Those who love the *Harry Potter* stories are no exception. Their passionate concern for the well-being of Harry and his friends, and their strong desire to see unpleasant characters such as Professor Snape 'redeemed' and brought fully into the fold of the good and heroic, proves that they have an inbuilt need to see goodness victorious. How close, though, does this story come to the biblical model that I have outlined above?

There is certainly one way in which Christian high ideals are not reflected in the *Harry Potter* books—just as they are not reflected in the everyday situations that many of us experience in real life. As many Christian critics have loudly protested, Harry and his friends do not attempt to bless their enemies and 'turn the other cheek' when they meet conflict, especially in their day-to-day relationship with nasty schoolmate Draco Malfoy. Hermione's advice is always to ignore Malfoy's repeated provocation but, for Ron in particular, corridor fights (using wands) are fairly commonplace whenever Gryffindor and Slytherin are timetabled for joint lessons. Even Harry, usually a peace-loving boy, finally succumbs to Malfoy's taunts in *The Order of the Phoenix* and lands several punches on him (what Professor McGonagall indignantly calls 'Muggle duelling', *OoP*, p. 367).

Even more seriously (as I mentioned previously), the simmering mutual hatred between Harry and Professor Snape continues un-abated in *The Order of the Phoenix*, and is beginning to harden into a fixed attitude of unforgiveness. Until this point in the story, there has been minimal emphasis on the idea that Harry himself might have to fight evil in the battleground of his own heart or mind, and it is unclear how this theme might develop in the last two books. J.K.Rowling has suggested that Harry will never be seriously tempted by the Dark Arts, which may be a deliberate attempt on her part to distance her narrative from the temptation theme that occurs so strongly in the *Star Wars* legend. Harry's hatred of Snape plays a pivotal role in *The Order of the Phoenix*, however, as I shall discuss further in the following few pages, and it seems to me that it will need to be properly resolved before the end of the saga.

These points aside, each of the biblical factors in the triumph of goodness that I have described appears as an important aspect of the *Harry Potter* stories, and we can trace how these factors are combined to bring good to a point of advantage over evil.

As two of the books in the series have yet to be published, the way in which Lord Voldemort will finally be defeated is known only to author J.K. Rowling—her readers can only speculate. However, the first five books provide indicators that good must triumph when evil is opposed with love, mercy towards evildoers, self-sacrifice even to the point of death, individual personal courage and strength of character, co-operation and unity between friends and allies, and help from more mysterious sources beyond the battling individual—all of which uphold to some extent the biblical models that I've outlined. There are also strong hints in the story that the very self-destructiveness of evil will play a part. The seeds of defeat are contained within evil actions and Lord Voldemort is often non-plussed by the fact that his evil seems to backfire on him.

SELF-SACRIFICE

As we have seen, a reading of *The Prisoner of Azkaban* undermines Karen Jo Gounaud's view that forgiveness and reconciliation play no part in the *Harry Potter* stories. Ms Gounaud also suggests, however, that 'the... action is within the context of who controls the magic, not self-sacrifice for such issues as faith, family and freedom.' She is mistaken here too, as the story is rooted in and develops from a single act of self-sacrifice for family and freedom. Harry's remarkable escape from Voldemort as a baby is not due to any special powers that Harry himself possesses at the time. When his mother Lily offers herself to Voldemort to be killed in Harry's place, a 'magic' that Voldemort does not foresee kicks into action. Once Lily has died, Voldemort of course tries to kill Harry, too, but, because of Lily's self-sacrifice, the lethal spell backfires, stripping Voldemort of his power and leaving Harry alive, but wounded on the forehead. The wound heals to form the lightning-shaped scar by which Harry is identified forever after. In *The Chamber of Secrets*, Voldemort (in the form of a 'memory' of his teenage self) admits that Lily Potter's self-sacrificial death had been 'a powerful counter-charm' to his killing curse. The Dark Lord thought he controlled the magic, but a mother's self-sacrifice wrested that control from him and proved too powerful for him to overcome.

It is probably worth mentioning here that Harry's lightning scar has been claimed by at least one Christian critic as a satanic symbol. The anonymous spokesman for Freedom Village USA supports his claim by quoting Jesus' words from Luke 10:18: 'I saw Satan fall like lightning from heaven.' This commentator forgets to mention that seven chapters later in Luke, Jesus compares his own second coming to a bolt of lightning (Luke 17:24). Also overlooked are the 44 other references to lightning in the (NIV) Bible, in which lightning is consistently used as a symbol of the power of God over evil. The idea of lightning as a symbol of Satan, therefore, is not credible when one looks at its use in scripture as a whole.

As well as the death of Lily Potter, there are further strong pointers in the story to the value of self-sacrifice as an antidote to evil. Towards the end of *The Philosopher's Stone*, the three children are racing to prevent the Stone from being stolen by Voldemort's agent and providing Voldemort with the means to attain immortality. Ron is masterminding and participating in a game of living chess, which has been set as an obstacle to the chamber containing the Stone itself. He reaches a point where he realizes, 'it's the only way… I've got to be taken'. When Harry and Hermione protest, he says, 'That's chess!… You've got to make some sacrifices!' Ron is knocked unconscious but succeeds in getting Harry and Hermione through to the next challenge (PS, p. 205).

An even stronger statement comes in Chapter 19 of *The Prisoner of Azkaban*. Peter Pettigrew, formerly one of James Potter's closest friends, is finally revealed as the villain who betrayed Harry's parents to their deaths. He tries to claim that he had no choice in the matter, saying that Voldemort would have killed him if he had refused to submit. The reply comes back from Remus Lupin, 'Then you should have died!… Died rather than betray your friends, as we would have done for you!' (p. 275). This is a piercing echo of Jesus' famous words, 'No one has greater love than this, to lay down one's life for one's friends' (John 15:13, NSRV). Any *Harry Potter* fan hearing this Bible verse for the first time would immediately associate it with Professor Lupin's words and would have this as a basis for understanding Jesus' self-sacrificial act, dying for others.

So, self-sacrifice is a weapon against evil to be found at the very core of the story, both in the overthrow of Voldemort at the outset and in the more mundane encounters with him throughout.

LOVE

John 15:13 clearly points to love as being the prime motivation for the act of dying for another person. Just so, the foundational act of self-sacrifice at the heart of the *Harry Potter* saga is also inspired purely by love. What is more, the effect of that love endures way beyond the initial act itself. In *The Philosopher's Stone*, we discover that the love for Harry that motivated Lily's sacrifice gave him a lingering protection that made it impossible for Voldemort, or anyone acting on his behalf, to touch Harry. Once Harry has obtained the Philosopher's Stone itself at the end of the first book, Quirrell tries to take it from him, but finds that his hands begin to blister when they are in contact with Harry's skin. Professor Dumbledore later explains to Harry, 'Your mother died to save you. If there is one thing Voldemort cannot understand, it is love... Quirrell, full of hatred, greed and ambition, sharing his soul with Voldemort, could not touch you for this reason. It was agony to touch a person marked by something so good' (PS, p. 216).

The importance of showing love towards all 'classes' of society equally also plays a large part in the story. A distinguishing feature of Voldemort and his evil followers is that they are violently prejudiced against Muggles (non-wizards) as well as wizards who have Muggle ancestry. In his choice of friendship with Ron rather than Malfoy (PS, p. 81), Harry shows his refusal to participate in this prejudice. Malfoy is the son of an influential pureblood family that despises Muggle-borns. Ron is also from a long line of pure-blood wizards, but the crucial difference is that his father is well known in the wizarding community as a 'Muggle-lover' who works hard in the Ministry of Magic to defend Muggle rights. Meanwhile, Hermione is often verbally abused by Draco because she is the daughter of two Muggle parents, but both Harry and Ron remain staunchly protective of her against Malfoy's offensive 'Mudblood' taunts.

The antagonism between those who follow Voldemort in wishing to wipe out Muggle-born wizards and those who are dedicated 'Muggle-lovers' is the driving force behind the plot of the second book, The Chamber of Secrets. How reminiscent of Jesus' refusal to keep 'in' with the powerful Pharisees of his day, preferring instead to keep company with men and women of humbler origins, as well as those who were considered outcasts from society, tainted by immorality or racial 'impurity'.

With The Order of the Phoenix, however, J.K. Rowling returns to the theme of love as a quality that Lord Voldemort can neither understand nor bear to encounter. The prophecy that identifies Harry as the only one able to destroy Voldemort includes the phrase 'he will have power the Dark Lord knows not' (OoP, p. 741). That power is love—described by Professor Dumbledore (in terms reminiscent of Song of Songs) as 'a force that is at once more wonderful and more terrible than death, than human intelligence, than the forces of nature' (*OoP*, p. 743)—the greatest of the subjects for study hidden in the Department of Mysteries at the Ministry of Magic. The fact that Harry possesses love 'in such quantities' and Voldemort has it 'not at all' is what saves Harry at the end of *The Order of the Phoenix*. We now wait to see what part it might play in the final overthrow of the Dark Lord.

MERCY

The power of evil and death has been conquered on Harry's behalf by another person in his babyhood, but, in the same way that we have to apply the victory of Christ in our everyday lives, Harry cannot just sit back in the complacent belief that there is nothing more to be done. On the contrary, he has to take hold of the advantage over Voldemort that his mother has won for him and apply it to the potentially destructive situations in which he finds himself.

In real-life conflict with everyday evil, one of the most important qualities that Jesus taught and modelled was that of mercy towards enemies. In *The Prisoner of Azkaban*, there is a seemingly minor incident that, according to Dumbledore, is likely to be pivotal in the outcome of the conflict between Harry and Lord Voldemort. Face to face with the traitor Peter Pettigrew, Harry is given the choice of whether or not to allow Sirius Black and Remus Lupin to take revenge on Pettigrew and kill him. Harry is sorely tempted to give in to the desire to see Pettigrew punished, but decides in the end to spare his life. Pettigrew escapes, to seek out Voldemort and re-enter his service.

After the event, Dumbledore praises Harry for his restraint and explains that when one wizard saves another's life, a lasting bond is created between them. Harry objects that he doesn't want a 'bond' with the man who betrayed his parents and expresses his concern that his leniency might have paved the way for Pettigrew to assist Voldemort's return. However, Dumbledore says, 'You have sent Voldemort a deputy who is in your debt... This is magic at its deepest, its most impenetrable, Harry. But trust me... the time may come when you will be very glad you saved Pettigrew's life' (*PoA*, p. 311).

It does indeed prove to be the case that both Pettigrew and Harry play roles in Voldemort's revival—Pettigrew by choice and Harry as an unwilling pawn—and it may seem at this stage in the story that for Harry to have allowed his foe to escape alive was weak and foolish of him. Yet, there is still Dumbledore's strong hint to consider, that the bond forged between the two characters by Harry's act of mercy will in some way prove crucial in the eventual downfall of Lord Voldemort.

For those who are familiar with Tolkien's *The Lord of the Rings*, a striking parallel to Harry's situation might come to mind. To avoid spoiling the story for those who are still to read it, I will simply ask a question. How different would the end of Frodo Baggins' quest have been if he and Sam had taken full advantage of their desire and the frequent opportunities they had to kill Gollum? Readers of the *Harry Potter* stories will have to wait and see exactly how the destruction of Voldemort's power is achieved, but there is every possibility that Harry's mercy towards Pettigrew—his supposed weakness and foolishness—will be the foundation of his victory.

THE SELF-DESTRUCTIVENESS OF EVIL

Lord Voldemort, as we have seen, is unaware that two of the three people he uses to aid his revival in *The Goblet of Fire* have a bond of goodness between them. Neither did Voldemort know that Lily Potter's self-sacrifice on behalf of her son would act as a counter-charm to his killing curse. When Harry confronts the newly restored Voldemort and sets off the linking of their wand lights that leads to Harry's one-in-a-million chance of escape, Voldemort's look of horror betrays the fact that this, too, is a turn of events that he did not foresee. I cannot read these accounts of the Dark Lord's ignorance without thinking immediately of *The Lion, the Witch and the Wardrobe*: Aslan's explanation of his return from death is that 'though the Witch knew the Deep Magic, there is a magic deeper still which she did not know'.[29] In the *Narnia Chronicles* and in the *Harry Potter* books, too, just as in the real-life cosmic battle, evil is always outwitted by the extravagant creativity of goodness.

In addition to the fact of Voldemort's ignorance of the greater power of goodness, there is the suggestion here that evil power must always eventually destroy the one who uses it. Not only is baby Harry left alive when Voldemort makes his initial attack, but the spell actually rebounds on the evil wizard, stripping him of his power and sending him into a humiliating 13-year retreat. Then, after his return to power in *The Goblet of Fire*, Voldemort is unnerved by the emergence from his wand of shadowy figures representing his most recent victims—figures that stand between him and Harry as Harry makes good his escape. Although these shadows are not ghosts but spell-echoes, I am reminded here of Shakespeare's *Richard III*, in which the ghosts of Richard's victims appear to him on the eve of battle and sap his confidence by reminding him of his guilt. Voldemort, too, quails under the knowledge that the evil he has done will not be forgotten: guilt is real and his own wand holds a damning record of his wrongs that cannot be erased.

Furthermore, many *Harry Potter* fans predict that the potion Voldemort uses for his restoration to power contains within it the seeds of his ultimate destruction. I, too, subscribe to this theory, that the bond between Harry and Pettigrew will be subtly at work within Voldemort's very being and eventually undermine his power to destroy Harry. The urge to preserve life will prove stronger than the desire to destroy it—an 'even deeper magic' that Voldemort will be powerless to combat. This is, of course, only speculation: we have to wait for the end of the story to be published before we will know exactly how Voldemort's defeat will be played out.

It is interesting that both C.S. Lewis and J.R.R. Tolkien seem to agree with the principle that evil consumes the one who uses it. In Lewis' *Voyage to Venus*, Dr Ransom realizes from his encounters with the Un-Man that 'bad men... [are] melted down into their Master, as a lead soldier slips down and loses his shape in the ladle held over the gas ring'.[30] In Tolkien's *The Lord of the Rings*, the One Ring confers absolute power on its user, but also, in time, causes that person literally to fade away into nothingness.

COURAGE

So far, we've seen the power of love, self-sacrifice, mercy, the self-destructiveness of evil and its inability to keep step with goodness all clearly portrayed in the *Harry Potter* stories. In addition, as Harry meets the various challenges presented to him by Voldemort's murderous intentions, a vital tool in his defeat of evil is his own rare courage and strength of character. Bravery is, of course, the defining quality of Gryffindor students at Hogwarts and Harry demonstrates it continually, in all his encounters with evil. Harry's courage is not bravado or recklessness—as he says ruefully in *The Prisoner of Azkaban*, 'I don't go looking for trouble. Trouble usually finds *me*' (p. 60). Instead, it is to do with the willingness to confront danger head-on and fight even when winning seems impossible, simply because fighting is the right thing to do, and with the most insignificant physical forces. It's this kind of courage that enables Harry to step out of hiding in Chapter 34 of *The Goblet of Fire* to pit his feeble disarming charm against Voldemort's seemingly unblock-able killing curse—an action that might be seen as his coming of age in the story so far. As Dumbledore assures him, 'You have shown bravery beyond anything I could have expected of you tonight, Harry... You have shouldered a grown wizard's burden and found yourself equal to it' (*GoF*, p. 606). This kind of courage—the courage of a David when faced with a Goliath—is seen in the story as a necessary characteristic in the fight against evil.

ASSISTANCE FROM OTHERS

Not everyone approves of Harry's bravery, however. Some Christians have objected that, in all his encounters with evil, Harry battles alone, giving readers the mistaken impression that we can conquer evil 'in our own strength'. In fact, this claim does not bear scrutiny. Although Harry alone is the focus of the climax to each episode (as one would expect from any story with a central hero figure), a very important element in his battles is always the help he receives from other sources, as Harry himself acknowledges (*OoP*, p. 293). In *The Philosopher's Stone*, his good friends Ron and Hermione play vital roles in bringing Harry through the series of obstacles guarding the chamber containing the Stone. Once there, Harry finds the Stone only because Dumbledore has previously explained to him how the Mirror of Erised works and Dumbledore himself physically rescues Harry from the chamber. In *The Prisoner of Azkaban*, once again Hermione's help in saving the lives of Buckbeak and Sirius Black is indispensable, and Professors Dumbledore, McGonagall and Lupin must all be credited with contributions to Harry's defeat of the Dementors. So, here we see Harry relying on the very simple practical help of his friends and teachers.

In the second and fourth books of the series, the help Harry receives is from a more mysterious external source, which is perhaps the closest the stories approach the idea of a more 'spiritual' dimension to life in the magical community. Halfway through *The Chamber of Secrets*, Professor Dumbledore, temporarily suspended from his position as Headmaster, says two things in Harry's hearing as he leaves. First, he says that he will never be truly absent from the school while people remain there who are loyal to him. Second, he promises that 'help will always be given at Hogwarts to those who ask for it' (p. 195). At the climax of the story, as Harry faces the basilisk in the chamber, controlled by Tom Riddle, he blurts out his strongly held belief that Dumbledore, not Voldemort, is the greatest wizard in the world. The consequence of this expression of loyalty is that Fawkes, Dumbledore's pet phoenix, flies singing into the chamber, carrying the school Sorting Hat. Then, as the basilisk lunges wildly at him, Harry mutters a frantic plea for help. He rams the Hat on to his head and pulls out from it a jewel-encrusted sword, with which he is able to put an end to the basilisk. Harry receives a lethal wound from the monster's fang in the process, but Fawkes heals the wound with his tears.

In *The Goblet of Fire*, once again it is the song of the phoenix ('the sound he associated with Dumbledore') that enables Harry to resist Voldemort to the point where he is able to break the wands' connection and run to safety. J.K. Rowling's book for Comic Relief, *Fantastic Beasts and Where to Find Them*,[31] explains the assistance that Harry gains from Fawkes: 'Phoenix song is magical: it is reputed to increase the courage of the pure of heart and to strike fear into the hearts of the impure' (p. 32). So here we have an interaction between the strength and purity of Harry's own character and an outside source of help (associated in a mysterious way with Dumbledore) that works together with Harry's qualities of character.

UNITY

As *The Goblet of Fire* draws to a close, a new and crucial factor in the battle against evil emerges—not just cooperation between friends but a unity of spirit that brings together even natural enemies in a common cause. Cornelius Fudge places himself and the Ministry of Magic in opposition to Dumbledore and Harry; Dumbledore responds by calling together the Order of the Phoenix, a band of people loyal to himself and dedicated to preventing the further advance of Voldemort's power. In his speech to Hogwarts School at the Leaving Feast, Dumbledore warns the students that Voldemort has a great 'gift for spreading discord and enmity' and impresses upon them, 'We are only as strong as we are united, as weak as we are divided' (*GoF*, p. 627).

At the beginning of the new term, the call for unity is re-emphasized again and again. Even the Sorting Hat, in a new song, bemoans the fact that it must split the school into houses at all (*OoP*, p. 186). Four of the Hogwarts staff are members of the Order of the Phoenix—Professors Dumbledore, McGonagall, Hagrid and Snape. As the story progresses, central to their struggle to prevent Voldemort from gaining a foothold is the urgent need for Harry to learn how to close his mind to the Dark Lord's attempted intrusions, and the teacher chosen to coach Harry in the necessary skills is Professor Snape. But Snape and Harry, though both on the same side in the battle, harbour a mutual hatred that leads to disaster. In his festering anger and resentment, Harry makes no real effort to learn Occlumency from Snape and, at a moment of crisis, fails to enlist Snape's help when it is most needed. As a consequence, Voldemort manages to lure Harry to the Department of Mysteries, where a desperate fight ends with the wounding of several of Harry's loyal friends and the death of his devoted godfather, Sirius Black.

Until *The Order of the Phoenix*, Harry has made no real mistakes in his encounters with Voldemort. When he does make an error of judgment, it is the direct result of disunity—the deep division between himself and Professor Snape, which has been left unresolved for five years. There are now two books in the series remaining, for the rift to be healed.

GOOD AND EVIL MAGIC?

This discussion would not be complete without an attempt to address the concerns of those Christians who criticize the whole premise of the good-versus-evil conflict in the *Harry Potter* stories on the grounds that the supposedly good characters are actually using evil (that is, supernatural, occult power) to battle evil. Quite apart from the fact that the magic in the *Harry Potter* books is not of a supernatural, occult nature, these Christians would do well to consider that, in all the battles between good and evil in the story, the ultimate source of victory is seen to be the moral virtues of the good characters, not the spells or magical objects or creatures that are used as tools in the conflict. So, for example, Harry uses the magical Mirror of Erised to find the Philosopher's Stone, but the mirror would not have given up the Stone to anyone whose object in seeking it was any form of self-gain. Harry's selflessness, coupled with the protection of his mother's love, was the basis of his success. In *The Chamber of Secrets*, it is Harry's outspoken faithfulness to Dumbledore that enables him to obtain the magical objects he needs, while in *The Prisoner of Azkaban*, one of the outstanding themes of the story is the necessity to confront and overcome crippling fear: the all-important Patronus charm works only when fear has been defeated. In the fourth book, *The Goblet of Fire*, Harry uses the only spell he can think of against Voldemort— in the full knowledge that the spell itself is powerless against him. Harry's raw courage in the face of death, his purity of heart and his passionate refusal to submit in any way to Voldemort's power are the qualities that give him the vital edge over the evil wizard, rather than the tools he uses in the process.

The Order of the Phoenix brings Harry close to defeat as he fails to learn the magic necessary to keep Voldemort at bay. Yet in the end it is his love for Sirius that banishes the Dark Lord once again (a love that presumably overrides even his hatred for Snape). 'In the end,' Dumbledore tells him, 'it mattered not that you could not close your mind. It was your heart that saved you' (*OoP*, p. 743).

IMPLICATIONS FOR TODAY

While traditional boundaries between personal moral goodness and evil become increasingly blurred in our society, there is still a recognition that some forces pose a real threat to our peace, safety and happiness in the world. The full extent of international drug trafficking, terrorism, domestic violence and governmental 'sleaze' would fall into this category, and their full extent is probably clearer to us now than ever before. We are also more aware of the parts played by the governments of Western, developed nations in exploiting the more unstable governments of developing nations for financial gain. We see huge evils in our world, but there is also a sense of powerlessness among ordinary citizens. What can we hope to do?

Fictional stories of good versus evil keep alive in their readers the knowledge that goodness can prevail. In the *Harry Potter* stories, we have just such examples, which have inspired imaginations right across the world, young and old. What is more, the stories go some way towards demonstrating some key elements in a Christian understanding of how goodness triumphs. Most important of all, the stories are built around an act of self-sacrificial death that readers are never allowed to forget, so fundamental is it to Harry's motivation and sense of purpose throughout his adventures.

This is fantasy, though. In the real world, whom do we see demonstrating the full combination of love, mercy, self-sacrifice, humility, courage, unity, reliance on friends and trust in a external source of help that responds to our cries and provides us with the tools to conquer evil? We, as Christians, should be the ones who are prepared to take up these weapons and risk everything, including opposition from both secular and religious sources, to storm the gates of hell. Readers of the *Harry Potter* books know that the strategy of no response adopted by Minister for Magic, Cornelius Fudge, is at best inadequate, at worst lethal. Denial of the presence and power of evil, as Dumbledore so adamantly insists, is not a viable option. Readers also know, from *The Order of the Phoenix*, that division among those who ought to be allies can be disastrous.

Christians also claim to recognize the need to stand together to fight evil. So, if the triumph of goodness ever steps out of the pages of a fantasy novel, to be clearly seen in real-life relationships in our streets, homes, offices and places of national and international power, perhaps the readers of the *Harry Potter* stories will see and recognize the heroism that so excites them—in the *united* Church of Jesus Christ. Or is this an impossible dream?

CHAPTER 5

TRUTH AND ILLUSION

Surely you desire truth in the inner parts.
PSALM 51:6

It made all the difference in the world, Harry.
You helped uncover the truth.
HARRY POTTER AND THE PRISONER OF AZKABAN, P. 310

One of the ideas that is most prominent in postmodern thought is that 'truth' does not exist as an absolute value for all people at all times and 'reality', similarly, is not an objective concept, independent of human perception. From a postmodern viewpoint, what's 'true' for you may not be 'true' for me—reality is fluid, subjectively and individually determined.

To see how this idea has developed over the past few years, it would be useful to look at some definitions taken from the *Concise Oxford Dictionary*. In the eighth edition, published in 1990, 'reality' is defined as 'what is real or existent or underlies appearances'. Almost a decade later, this definition has become outdated: the ninth (1999) edition of the same dictionary omits any mention of a reality 'underlying appearances', preferring to talk of 'a thing that is actually experienced or seen'. The new, postmodernist way of looking at the world claims that nothing 'underlies appearances'— our perception of the surface of things (what we 'actually experience or see') is the only reality. As the surface appearance of the world may present itself differently according to a person's point of view, 'reality' then becomes a matter of individual perception at any one time.

This being the case, the 1990 dictionary's second definition of the word 'true'—'genuine... not spurious or counterfeit'— becomes objectively meaningless (and it is, indeed, missing from the 1999 edition). The idea of genuineness depends for its sense on the acknowledgment of a reality separate from appearances, which postmodernism rejects. In the new way of thinking, a counterfeit might be considered every bit as valid as the object it is a copy of, so that one is no more 'true' than the other.

The implications of this shift away from belief in an objective truth that may be hidden from view but nonetheless 'real', and towards the equal acceptance of surface appearance and subjective, changeable perceptions, are far-reaching. Most particularly, it is commonly accepted, in these days of visual media and the cult of the celebrity, that a person's worth may be judged by their outward appearance—the 'image' they present to the world—rather than by their inner character. This has led to the assumption that outwardly visible signs of youth, beauty and style are more to be desired than, say, the hidden wisdom that might come from long life and experience. Some national newspapers and magazines delight in gloating over photographs of well-known entertainers out on the street looking less than their best, as if this devalues them as people. This message, repeated constantly in the media, may have a powerful influence on those ordinary members of society who are not in the public eye, especially young people who are in the process of discovering and shaping their sense of identity in the world. There is enormous pressure on children and teenagers to 'improve' themselves in terms of their physical appearance rather than the inner qualities that are not immediately apparent to casual observers.

Entertainers are in the business of creating an image on stage or in front of the cameras—a fantasy world—in order to evoke pleasant emotions in their audience for a short period of time and just for fun. We might feel a little uneasy when the media try to extend this fantasy image to envelop the private 'real' life of the performer. It is perhaps more alarming, though, to realize that politicians now commonly employ image consultants to enable them to create a more favourable impression on the electorate and so influence public opinion on matters of major social concern. A society that confuses a soothing voice or winning smile with genuine honesty or devotion to the public good is in serious trouble. It's at this point that image-making becomes deception and trust breaks down.

Of course, deception is not a postmodernist invention. People have always spoken lies in order to get themselves out of trouble or others into it. Words are a powerful tool for manipulating other people's thoughts, creating false, distorted or misleading impressions of reality. In our personal relationships, we are badly hurt by hypocrisy and betrayal from trusted friends and family members. To be lied to by such people, or to discover that our trust in them is in any way misplaced, is a deeply humiliating experience. We know that someone in our close circle of friends who deliberately pretends to be something other than what they 'really' are is a bad person; and the other side of the coin is that when we ourselves succumb to the pressure to project a public image that is very different from our inner self, we can become ill at ease and confused about our true identity.

We also recognize that judging by appearances alone is the basis for racism and other types of prejudice that cause suffering and injustice in society. So we do know that there always has been, and always will be, a need to discern between truth and falsehood in others and ourselves. Despite the postmodernist influence of the media, we seem to have a deep-seated need for a reality that underlies appearances.

THE WORD OF GOD

At least at first sight, the biblical worldview is in direct opposition to postmodernist theory on this issue. In his prayer for the disciples before his death, Jesus said to the Father, 'your word is truth' (John 17:17). If we consider these four short words along with other scripture, they have staggering implications. The Prologue to John's Gospel states that the word of God brought about the creation of the world (John 1:3), while Hebrews 1:3 speaks of Jesus 'sustaining all things by his powerful word'. Truth, given substance as the spoken, living word of God, is therefore a foundation stone for the created order—the power that holds the universe together, solid, fixed and all-encompassing.

Something of the power of truth can also be seen in those passages of scripture that describe the word of God as a terrifying weapon. Jeremiah spoke against the false prophets of his day who prophesied the comforting, wishy-washy 'delusions of their own minds' with the rebuke, '"Is not my word like fire," declares the Lord, "and like a hammer that breaks a rock in pieces?"' (Jeremiah 23:26, 29). The author of Hebrews had a similar insight when he described the word of God as 'sharper than any double-edged sword...' (Hebrews 4:12). A raging fire, a sledgehammer, a double-edged sword—these are pictures of truth as a formidable force that can overcome any resistance.

Truth not only consumes, shatters and pierces evil, however: it also has the power to liberate those who are willing to recognize and embrace it. Jesus said to his loyal disciples, 'You will know the truth, and the truth will set you free' (John 8:32), but our own willingness to accept the truth is vital to that freedom. In our attempts to deepen our personal relationship with God, we can make no progress at all if we are not willing to deal with him in transparent honesty. As Psalm 51:6 says, God demands 'truth in the inner parts'. Yet, we instinctively try to hide from him when we know that we have done wrong or when we are troubled by something that is damaging our lives: Adam and Eve's first reaction to the realization that they had disobeyed God's command was to cover up parts of their physical bodies, then hide from God himself. Equally, John 3:20–21 (NRSV) says, 'For all who do evil hate the light and do not come to the light, so that their deeds may not be exposed. But those who do what is true come to the light…' The word of God, which is truth, has the power to bring hidden things to light.

To return to the biblical image of the word of God as a double-edged sword, Hebrews 4:12 says that the function of the sword is to pierce 'even to dividing soul and spirit… it judges the thoughts and attitudes of the heart. Nothing in all creation is hidden from God's sight'. God sees through us, so it is useless to try to hide anything about ourselves. A far more positive response to the probing of the double-edged sword is open confession, because from that comes healing.

THE LIES OF SATAN

As truth is so fundamental a part of God's nature, it is clear that falsehood is bound to be fiercely opposed by him. Satan himself was described by Jesus as 'a liar and the father of lies' (John 8:44), and 'You shall not give false testimony against your neighbour' (Exodus 20:16) was one of the ten commandments that formed the bedrock of the Israelites' understanding of right relationships between themselves, God and other people. If truth demands openness and willing exposure to the light of God, falsehood has to do with hiding from God, darkness and slavery. The prophet Isaiah said to the rulers of Jerusalem that they had 'made a lie their refuge and falsehood their hiding-place'. No doubt the rulers felt safe hidden behind their lies, but Isaiah went on to warn them that God would 'sweep away' that refuge and hiding-place in a terrible hailstorm (Isaiah 28:15, 17). This is just one more example of the way God powerfully opposes falsehood with truth.

Lies are a major part of the very nature of evil and, according to American psychiatrist M. Scott Peck, the refusal to face the truth about oneself and one's circumstances is a primary contributor to mental illness. Dr Peck asserts that 'mental health is an ongoing process of dedication to reality at all costs'[32]—the reality disputed by postmodernism. His book *People of the Lie*[33] is a convincing exploration of the ways in which human evil is inextricably linked with the habit of lying to others and to oneself.

SPEAKING THE TRUTH

The truth that comes from the word of God, then, has tremendous power—to break apart and heal, shine light into dark places and pierce to the heart. When we speak the truth, we need to be aware that our speech may unleash a similar power. This is perhaps why, although the Bible forbids lying and deception, it does not command us to speak the truth, the whole truth and nothing but the truth at all times without thought for its effects on those who hear it. In Ephesians 4:15, Paul emphasizes 'speaking the truth *in love*' as an aid to Christian maturity and unity, and this is perhaps a key. Many of us know from experience that truth spoken without love can be merely destructive, causing deep, long-lasting damage to relationships between people (although we may accept painful truths more readily from someone of whose love we are absolutely sure). Jesus said to his disciples, just before his death, 'I have much more to say to you, more than you can now bear. But when he, the Spirit of truth, comes, he will guide you into all truth' (John 16:12–13). This suggests that we are justified in withholding 'all truth' from others until it is appropriate for them to hear it (and it may be that, as people increase in maturity, they also increase in the amount of truth they can handle).

For this reason, we are also allowed to keep other people's confidences. Proverbs 11:13 says, 'A gossip betrays a confidence, but a trustworthy man keeps a secret.' Trustworthiness is a Christian virtue to which we should aspire, and this may mean withholding truth from certain people at certain times. It is for us to discern what is appropriate in such circumstances.

DISCERNING THE TRUTH

We might think that if truth (or goodness) and falsehood (or evil) are so diametrically opposed to each other in the biblical worldview, they should be easily distinguishable from one another. This is certainly not the case. On the contrary, the Bible makes it clear that discerning the truth about a person's character or their spiritual qualities is often very difficult indeed. Paul tells us, 'Satan himself masquerades as an angel of light. It is not surprising, then, if his servants masquerade as servants of righteousness' (2 Corinthians 11:14–15). Thus evil can be wrongly perceived as goodness.

It is perhaps more surprising, though, to realize that good may also be mistaken for evil. Jeremiah was constantly at odds with fellow prophets who claimed that the Israelites were not going to be sent into exile. Rex Mason, in his *People's Bible Commentary* on Jeremiah,[34] makes the interesting point that these false prophets based their message of peace and security on the accepted scriptural truth that Jerusalem was under divine protection and could never be shaken (see Psalm 125:1, for example). To their way of thinking, Jeremiah was prophesying against the revealed word of God and therefore speaking evil. Bearing in mind that many Christians today would say that a basic test of contemporary prophecy is whether or not it is supported by scripture, we can understand why the Israelites of Jeremiah's time might have been confused.

The Gospels show that there were even those who heard and saw Christ's teaching and miracles, yet came to the conclusion that the spirit behind his power was demonic, that he was 'demon-possessed and raving mad' (John 10:20). If Christ himself—the purest embodiment of truth and goodness—appeared evil to some (in fact, to those religious leaders who might have been expected to recognize the work of God when they witnessed it), we cannot expect truth to be always obvious in our own experience.

Jesus did give a hint, however, as to how we might distinguish reality from counterfeit. He used the image of a flock of sheep that know their own shepherd's voice and will refuse to follow a stranger who is unfamiliar to them (John 10:4–5). Perhaps this suggests that discernment between truth and falsehood, good and evil, has less to do with a set of logical principles than a relationship with a person whose character we may trust implicitly.

DECEPTIVE APPEARANCES

The Bible has plenty to say on the subject of surface appearance versus underlying reality, and the conclusion reached is that where there is a difference between the two, it is of paramount importance. The prophet Samuel learnt an important lesson from God when he went to anoint one of the sons of Jesse as the next king of Israel. In his eyes, any of the seven oldest sons might have looked the part—they were all tall, strong and handsome—yet God 'rejected' them all. God's explanation of his choice of David, the overlooked youngest brother, was, 'Man looks at the outward appearance, but the Lord looks at the heart' (1 Samuel 16:7).

At the time of Jesus, the Pharisees (some of whom were those who judged Jesus to be evil) did not make the mistake of thinking that physical attractiveness was the key to God's favour. They believed, correctly, that God demanded righteousness, but they still earned some harsh words of condemnation from Jesus because they valued the outward appearance of righteousness above true goodness of the heart. Their 'righteousness' was a mere pretence, an outward display of rule-keeping, an image with no real substance, so Jesus denounced them as 'whitewashed tombs, which look beautiful on the outside but on the inside are full of dead men's bones...' (Matthew 23:27). Pretence was anathema to Jesus. He looked for outward behaviour that was consistent with a person's inner motivation, their attitude of heart.

As followers of Christ, we have no excuse for bigotry or prejudice of any kind, which springs from the tendency to judge others by their outward appearance. We need to allow for the fact that the 'heart' of another person may be much better or worse than the image they display. Indeed, no human being has the necessary depth of knowledge of another person's 'heart' to pass accurate judgment on their character. Only God can see clearly beyond the physical appearance or projected image of outward behaviour to the essence of a person's being. The Bible even suggests that we may be unaware of our own true inner being: 'The heart is deceitful above all things and beyond cure. Who can understand it?' (Jeremiah 17:9). It is the task of a lifetime for each one of us, in partnership with God, to shape a character in which our outward behaviour and the attitude of our heart reflect one another consistently and without a trace of pretence or contradiction.

DOWN TO EARTH

There is one more thing to be said here about the relative values of image and reality in the biblical worldview. We've been thinking of truth as a powerful spiritual force and a person's true character as something that may not be outwardly visible, but this does not mean that reality in the biblical worldview is necessarily an ephemeral, 'spiritual', intangible quality. If this were the case, we might be tempted to think that our inner hopes and dreams are of more value in our Christian experience than the everyday activities that we carry out in our physical environment. Proverbs 28:19, in typically down-to-earth fashion, gives us a rather stark warning: 'He who works his land will have abundant food, but the one who chases fantasies will have his fill of poverty.' This is not to say that all fantasy is wrong in God's eyes or that 'escapism' in the form of fictional literature, films or TV entertainment is forbidden to us. The pleasure we find in the world of the imagination is one of God's gifts to us. This verse simply serves to underline that God does not want us to become so heavenly minded that we're no earthly good. Rather, he wants us to live in the solid, earthy reality of the here-and-now, living out the truth of his word in our day-to-day working lives, with the people placed immediately around us. In this way we will learn best how to be authentic people who do not have to pretend to be anything other than our true selves.

So Christian belief holds up truth as a fundamental part of God's nature and vital for the preservation of our own well-being. It also makes a sharp distinction between image and substance, claiming that reality does exist as a separate entity to the surface appearance and, where appearances are different from the 'heart' of a person, it is the heart that must be taken into account. In the biblical world, also, truth can be notoriously difficult to tell apart from falsehood and we need to use careful discernment when faced with situations where a judgment needs to be made.

In a world that gives the subtle impression that 'truth' does not exist and cannot be known, where do the *Harry Potter* stories fit into the picture?

HARRY'S QUEST FOR TRUTH

Perhaps one of the reasons why the *Harry Potter* story appeals to such a wide range of people across the world is that it includes elements of many different literary genres. It's an old-fashioned boarding-school story, a tale of myth and magic, a classic good-versus-evil saga, an adventure story full of suspense and excitement, and also a detective story and a mystery. Each of the first four instalments is an individual whodunnit. In *The Philosopher's Stone*, we want to know who is trying to steal the Stone, while in *The Chamber of Secrets* the question is, 'Who is the Heir of Slytherin and who has opened the chamber?' *The Prisoner of Azkaban* revolves around the need to discover who really betrayed Harry's parents, while in *The Goblet of Fire* the race is on to identify the hidden servant of Voldemort who has infiltrated Hogwarts School. In all of these individual tales, the main thrust of the plot is towards uncovering deception and revealing truth.

Moreover, there is a sense in which the whole sweep of the saga is a quest to discover the truth about Harry's identity and his potential role in bringing Voldemort's power to a conclusive end. Each of the separate stories reveals more of the pieces necessary to provide a complete answer to this overarching mystery, and *The Order of the Phoenix*, with its revelation of Trelawny's first prophecy, fits an especially large piece into the puzzle. This means that, as with all such novels, a commitment to the idea that the truth really exists, waiting to be discovered, is absolutely vital to the success of the story. It simply would not work without that fixed point—the full truth about Harry and his circumstances, known to the author but glimpsed only partially by us, the readers, and by Harry himself within the story.

TRUTH AND FREEDOM

In several episodes dotted throughout the books, we see the power of truth to change Harry's circumstances and attitudes for the better. The first such episode takes place early on in *The Philosopher's Stone*.

Harry's entire life from the age of 15 months to 11 years is a lie, imposed on him by his aunt and uncle, who tell him that his parents died in a car crash and reveal nothing to him of his real identity as a wizard. The Dursleys, in their fear, hatred and latent jealousy of their nephew, find security for themselves in the lies that they have told him. The pretence means that they avoid the effort of extending their horizons beyond their 'normal', comfortable suburban existence, but that security is at the cost of imprisoning Harry behind walls of deceit. The name of the secondary school that Harry is due to attend, 'Stonewall High', says it all: his captivity is set to continue into his adulthood as the Dursleys refuse to face reality. Thankfully, the sudden arrival of Hagrid, smashing down the door of the Hut-on-the-Rock at the stroke of midnight on Harry's birthday to deliver his Hogwarts letter in person, brings a flash flood of truth that, for the Dursleys, sweeps away the lie in which they have been taking refuge and, for Harry, shatters the 'high stone walls' and sets him free to take his rightful place in the world to which he really belongs.

Harry learns more about the liberating power of truth during later events, in which the advice and example of Professor Dumbledore are highly influential. At the end of *The Prisoner of Azkaban*, Harry is kicking himself about the fact that he has allowed Pettigrew to get away—convinced that he has changed nothing for the better. Dumbledore reassures him that his actions 'made all the difference in the world... You helped uncover the truth' (*PoA*, p. 310). Harry is being reminded that he has revealed Sirius Black's innocence and thus made it possible for Sirius to be released from condemnation at a later date (although, sadly, Sirius dies before his name can be cleared). The truth is important for its own sake: even if its effects are not immediately apparent, it is always worth bringing to light, especially when it provides the chance to bring about justice for others.

Again, Harry benefits from Dumbledore's commitment to truth at the end of *The Goblet of Fire*, after his traumatic encounter with Voldemort. As we have noted before, Cornelius Fudge wishes to cover up Voldemort's return to avoid spreading panic throughout the wizard community, but Dumbledore refuses to hide the facts from his students: 'The Ministry of Magic... does not wish me to tell you this... It is my belief, however, that the truth is generally preferable to lies' (*GoF*, p. 626). Dumbledore tells the whole school that Voldemort has returned, that he murdered Cedric Diggory and that Harry escaped from him. The effect on Harry of this public explanation is noteworthy: 'Harry felt as though Dumbledore's speech at the Leaving Feast had unblocked him, somehow' (*GoF*, pp. 629–630). This unblocking, this release, gives Harry strength to come to terms with past events and look to the future without a sense of paralysing dread: 'what would come, would come... and he would have to meet it when it did' (*GoF*, p. 636).

The story also raises the suggestion, however, that truth is too potent to be bandied around without thought for its consequences. When Harry pleads to be told 'the truth' about everything from his past that has been concealed by the Dursleys, Dumbledore refuses to answer all his questions, saying, 'The truth... It is a beautiful and terrible thing, and should therefore be treated with great caution... I shall not, of course, lie' (PS, p. 216). Dumbledore knows that Harry will be able to bear more of the truth as he becomes more mature: 'When you are older... when you are ready, you will know' (PS, p. 216). Of course, the judgment of when exactly Harry might be ready for the responsibility that the truth will bring is a very difficult one for Dumbledore to make. At the end of The Order of the Phoenix, as Harry stands in the Headmaster's office beside himself with frustration and rage at the seeming injustice of his lot in life, Dumbledore confesses that he should not have withheld the answers to Harry's question for quite so long. We, in real life, might be thankful that the 'Spirit of truth' mentioned by Jesus in John 16:13 surely knows precisely the right time to speak in every situation.

TRUTH AND IRONY

The knowledge of truth is not only powerful within the story itself; it is a prime ingredient in the enjoyable excitement that readers feel as they immerse themselves in the narrative. The literary device of 'dramatic irony', used by countless authors since the days of the Greek classics such as Oedipus, depends for its effect on the presence of truths known to the reader but not to the characters themselves. At its simplest, it is the device that has children shouting, 'He's behind you!' at a pantomime. On a first reading of the Harry Potter books, we know only as much as Harry does as we follow him through the unravelling of the mystery; but a second reading, when we know how the plot ends, shows up all the clues that we missed along the way and provides buckets of dramatic irony.

The most breathtaking example occurs in The Goblet of Fire when Harry, trapped by his foot in a vanishing step on the staircase, drops the magical Marauder's Map, which shows by name the location of every person in the castle. Professors Snape and (faux) Moody are also present, and Moody is the one who picks up the map (which, unknown to the others, is showing the name 'Barty Crouch' on the exact spot where he is standing). On our first reading of the book, we do not know that Moody is an imposter, so we think little of the incident, but, on a second reading, that map, lying face-down on the floor, is like a stick of truth-dynamite waiting to explode. A lie incarnate is standing before us and we are practically shouting at Snape, like those children at the pantomime, to pick up the map that has the power to pierce through Moody's pretence and bring Voldemort's schemes crashing to the ground.

HARRY'S LIES

It has to be said, it is not the case that the bad guys in the *Harry Potter* stories are the liars and the good characters always speak the truth. A criticism levelled at Harry by almost all the Christian protestors is that he is a bad role model for young people because he tells lies to get himself out of trouble. One commonsense answer to this is that no one needs Harry Potter to teach them to tell lies. We all do it instinctively at an early age: it is part of our fallen nature. My family has an amusing story about my younger brother who, at the age of two, spent a happy afternoon filling our father's Wellington boots to the brim with mud from the garden. When challenged about this misdemeanour, he lifted an angelic face and said, 'Lisa did it!' If a storybook 13-year-old boy never told a lie to evade punishment, we would think him most unrealistic.

Of course, the real question is, are readers of the *Harry Potter* books being encouraged to believe that lying is acceptable behaviour? I think not. Harry does tell lies under pressure, but it is clear that he always feels uncomfortable about it. We never get the impression that he is being clever or admirable by deceiving others, and in this respect he contrasts vividly with the heroine of Philip Pullman's *His Dark Materials* trilogy, Lyra Belacqua, whose ability to lie convincingly and with ease is portrayed by Pullman as a character strength (at least, in the first two books of the series).

It is also fascinating to note that Harry's willingness to lie varies according to the moral quality of the person who is addressing him and his sense of security, or otherwise, in that person's presence. There is an excruciating scene in *The Prisoner of Azkaban* when Harry has been caught in the village of Hogsmeade without the necessary permission. Under questioning from Professor Snape, he lies frantically and repeatedly and escapes scrutiny only when he is rescued by Ron and Professor Lupin. Harry is ill at ease with Snape because he knows that Snape hates him, so he is very unwilling to entrust Snape with the truth about his feelings and actions.

With Professor Dumbledore in other scenes, however, it is a different matter. We are told that the Headmaster has a 'characteristic, piercing look' that 'always made Harry feel as though Dumbledore was seeing right through him' (*GoF*, p. 522). As well as this uncomfortable awareness that his motives are laid bare before Dumbledore's gaze, Harry has such a high regard for and trust in him that he feels more shame, and yet more desire to confess the truth, when asked by Dumbledore to give an explanation for wrongdoing (see *CoS*, p. 64, where Harry has to account for the crashing of Mr Weasley's flying car).

I am reminded here of the fact that in the *Narnia Chronicles*, characters feel compelled to tell the truth, however painful, when Aslan demands any explanations from them (for example, Jill Pole's confession of 'showing off' in *The Silver Chair*, pp. 27–28). It is as if the presence of extreme goodness, such as that shown by Aslan and, perhaps to a slightly lesser extent, by Dumbledore, draws the full truth out of people. This is not to diminish the fact that we are responsible for our choices between right and wrong, but it does turn the spotlight in two directions at once. Perhaps all of us who claim a Christian faith should ask ourselves whether or not we are the kind of people who so radiate the peace, grace and goodness of God that others are too ashamed to tell us lies and respect us enough to entrust us with difficult truths.

APPEARANCES AND REALITY

Another common criticism of the *Harry Potter* books is that good and evil characters are not easily distinguished from one another—that the two qualities are mixed together in a way that muddles right and wrong into shades of grey. These critics have missed the point quite spectacularly. As we have seen, the Bible itself demonstrates that good and evil, truth and falsehood, always present themselves ambiguously in human behaviour and it is up to the observer to learn how to discern between them. In the *Harry Potter* stories, the vast majority of the characters are a moral mixture, just as in real life, but there are some who deliberately disguise their evil intentions and others who suffer prejudice due to some outward characteristic that makes them seem less admirable than they really are. In all of these contradictions, J.K. Rowling is not aiming to confuse and corrupt her readers' moral judgment—quite the opposite. She expects us to recognize that outward appearances are deceptive and that it is vital to look behind those appearances, to the truth within. In this, she is in line with our everyday experience of reality and the biblical worldview.

A prime example of a good man who is misjudged because of his appearance and a 'disability' that is beyond his control is Professor Remus Lupin. The children's first sight of him is on the journey to Hogwarts for their third year, where he is asleep on the train. He is shabbily dressed, youngish but prematurely grey and frail in appearance: 'He looks like one good hex would finish him off', is Ron's comment on discovering that this is to be their new Defence Against the Dark Arts teacher (*PoA*, p. 60). Yet, Lupin proves to be the best DADA teacher that Harry and his friends have had, as well as a valuable personal mentor to Harry. Not until the end of *The Prisoner of Azkaban* do they discover the reason for Lupin's faded appearance: as a werewolf since childhood, he has been an outcast from normal society, unable to hold down a regular job. (His position at Hogwarts depends on a newly discovered antidote potion, which he has to drink at every full moon.) Lupin suffers as a result of other people's fear and prejudice, but at heart he is one of the most lovable characters in the story.

In general terms, however, there is also a thread running throughout the story dealing with a more serious kind of bigotry. In Chapter 4, I noted that there are two main 'classes' of wizards in Harry's world: 'purebloods' are wizards born of wizarding parents, while 'Muggle-borns' are those whose parents are not wizards. Some pureblood wizards—including Cornelius Fudge, the Minister for Magic, and Lucius Malfoy, father of Draco—are, to varying degrees, contemptuous of Muggle-borns, while Voldemort (himself only half-blood) has a pathological hatred of them. By contrast, we discover in *The Goblet of Fire* that pureblood Arthur Weasley's reputation as a 'Muggle-lover' has held him back from being promoted within the Ministry of Magic and caused his large family considerable hardship, but he is prepared to sacrifice status and wealth quietly for the sake of maintaining his admirable personal standards. There is a serious message here that high moral principles are not necessarily reflected by outward show or recognized with honour by other members of the community.

Another dangerously deceitful character is flamboyant DADA teacher Gilderoy Lockhart, who presents a charming 'celebrity' face to the world as the author of bestselling books about how to fight the Dark Arts. However, he proves to be a liar and a coward when called on to confront the monster in the chamber of secrets and save Ginny Weasley's life. Even the pictures of himself that line his office walls try to hide when they're revealed in the middle of the night with curlers in their hair! As his name suggests, the professor's gilded exterior conceals a completely locked heart.

Among the bad characters who deceive us into thinking that they are good, the most 'successful' in achieving their evil aims are those whose whole lives are a pretence—notably Peter Pettigrew and Barty Crouch Jr. Pettigrew, after betraying James and Lily Potter and faking his own death in a confrontation with Sirius Black (leaving Sirius to be imprisoned for his supposed murder), assumes the form of a rat and lives with Ron Weasley's family as a pet for the next 12 years.

The true identity of Scabbers the rat is dramatically revealed towards the end of *The Prisoner of Azkaban*, but events conspire to allow him to escape and rejoin Voldemort's service.

Even more devastating in effect is the pretence of Barty Crouch Jr who, like Pettigrew, is believed to be dead. He manages to infiltrate Hogwarts School, not in helpless animal form but in the guise of another living person—Mad-Eye Moody. Crouch's disguise is so impenetrable that he is able to guide Harry unerringly to the meeting with Voldemort that allows the Dark Lord to be restored to power and very nearly causes Harry's death. However, Harry's unexpected return from the confrontation unnerves faux Moody, forcing him to overplay his hand and act very slightly out of character. This slip is enough to alert Professor Dumbledore who, until this point, has been just as badly deceived as everyone else. The way in which Dumbledore rumbles Crouch's secret in time to rescue Harry from him is extremely enlightening: he is able to spot the counterfeit Moody because he is so very familiar with the true character of the real one. His explanation is, 'The real Moody would not have removed you from my sight after what happened tonight. The moment he took you, I knew—and I followed' (*GoF*, p. 590). It is the implicit trust and unity of purpose between Dumbledore and his friend, tried and tested over many years of acquaintance, that allows the Headmaster to distinguish truth from falsehood, reality from counterfeit.

HARRY'S DISCERNMENT OF TRUTH

J.K. Rowling shows us, then, the fact that truth and falsehood are often almost impossible to tell apart and the discernment that Dumbledore demonstrates is something that comes with experience. In *The Goblet of Fire*, we observe Harry starting to assess the true motivations of other people in a way that he has rarely done before. For example, on meeting Igor Karkaroff, Headmaster of Durmstrang School, 'Harry noticed that his smile did not extend to his eyes, which remained cold and shrewd' (*GoF*, p. 217). He is also confused by Mad-Eye Moody in a way that causes him to stop and think: 'Moody scared him slightly... yet Moody had just helped him avoid an awful lot of trouble' (*GoF*, p. 413). With his increasing maturity, Harry is learning never to assume that he can tell all there is to know about a person by appearances alone.

Finally, there is another lesson for Harry to learn at Hogwarts—that the depths of his own heart may be the hardest of all to discern and understand. The lesson begins in the first book in the series, *The Philosopher's Stone*, when Harry discovers the Mirror of Erised and visits it repeatedly at night-time to gaze at the 'reflection' of himself with the parents he has never known. Albus Dumbledore finds him there and gives him some advice that might at first seem a little bemusing, after all we have seen about the importance of looking at the heart rather than outward appearances. Although the mirror is showing Harry the deepest desire of his heart, Dumbledore warns him away from it, saying, '... this mirror will give us neither knowledge or truth. Men have wasted away in front of it, entranced by what they have seen, or been driven mad, not knowing if what it shows is real or even possible... It does not do to dwell on dreams and forget to live...' (*PS*, p. 157). Dumbledore is aware that 'the heart is deceitful above all things' and that dreams—even true, heartfelt, beautiful dreams—are not as important as living life in the here-and-now, making the most of the time and tools that are set before us, thinking also of the needs of others, 'working our land' instead of 'chasing fantasies'.

By the end of *The Goblet of Fire*, there are signs that Harry has listened to Dumbledore's wise advice. Faced with the choice between being declared the outright winner of the Triwizard Tournament or sharing the prize with Cedric Diggory, the image of himself holding the cup, walking out to the cheers of the crowd (and the admiration of one particular girl), takes a powerful hold on Harry's heart—but the story goes on to say, 'Then the picture faded...' and Harry agrees to share the honour with his schoolmate, who has in all fairness tied with him for first place.

IMPLICATIONS FOR TODAY

From the moment when the Dursleys' lies about his past are blown apart on his eleventh birthday, Harry matures in the knowledge that truth is powerful enough to both destroy and heal; surface appearance is not anywhere near as valid as underlying realities; a counterfeit is not the same as the genuine article and may be downright dangerous; the truth of another person's heart is not immediately apparent to a casual observer; and even the most genuine desires of his own heart must be carefully examined to discern where they might lead. Set against these messages from the *Harry Potter* books, which are all far closer to the biblical worldview than the prevailing current of postmodern thinking thrust on us from every side by today's media, the idea that the books encourage young people to perceive lies and deception as harmless fun begins to look ridiculous.

It is all too easy for the Church to lay a charge like this carelessly at the feet of a fictional schoolboy, and I hope I have shown that it is without foundation. Instead we should be taking the more difficult step of ensuring that we ourselves, as followers of a God who deeply loathes pretence and hypocrisy, are demonstrating transparent consistency between the image we present to the world and the attitude of our hearts, as well as developing trustworthiness, wise discernment in our dealings with other people and an openness to recognize and act on the truth of God's word when he speaks to us. If the Church is to present an effective witness to the world outside it, we need to surpass even Professor Albus Dumbledore's devotion to truth, in words and actions.

CHAPTER 6

POWER AND AUTHORITY

The rulers of the Gentiles lord it over them, and their high officials exercise authority over them. Not so with you.
MATTHEW 20:25

If you want to know what a man's like, take a good look at how he treats his inferiors, not his equals.
HARRY POTTER AND THE GOBLET OF FIRE, P. 456

A comparison of dictionary definitions will show that the concepts of power and authority are closely related to one another, although there is an important difference between them as well as similarities.

In the *Collins Concise Dictionary*, 'power' is defined first, and most simply, as 'the ability to do something' or, more specifically, as a 'political, financial, social... force or influence', while 'authority' is defined first as 'the power or right to control, judge or prohibit the actions of others'. The crucial difference here is that power is the mere *ability* to act as a ruler or judge in relation to other people, whereas authority is the *right* to act in that way.

This means that power can be accumulated by a person for his or her own use and used legitimately to benefit others, but it can also be seized by force and imposed destructively on others who are relatively powerless. Authority must usually be conferred on a person (whether that is by another person, an institution or simply as a result of experience and expert knowledge) and, just as importantly, must be freely recognized and acknowledged by others before it can take full effect in their experience. Authority is a two-way contract.

The vital similarity, though, is that both power and authority can be used to bring other people under control—and control can be both a useful aid to an ordered society and a great danger to personal freedom.

It seems clear that most people will happily pursue the goal of gaining power over others, but the idea of being overpowered by someone else is one that frightens us all. (This fear is at the heart of the power struggles that we might observe in every group of people who interact together.) Similarly, positions of authority are highly sought after, but the thought of submitting to authority exercised by another person or institution is not nearly so popular. In today's postmodern society, we are less willing than previous generations to acknowledge another person's or organization's 'right to control, judge or prohibit' our actions, for the very reason that we fear the power that they might be trying to exert over us. It is still true, however, that we recognize as 'natural leaders' those people who have the gift of inspiring others to trust wholeheartedly in their leadership and follow willingly in their footsteps.

The obvious danger in following a leader lies in the fact that those who wield power and authority are not always 'good' people. If we look at the governments of the world over the last century, we can see the rise and fall of many cruel dictators to whom human life and freedom have been cheap, who have used their power to impoverish, enslave and murder their subjects—and some of those dictators, such as Adolf Hitler, have been remarkably charismatic, persuasive leaders who have inspired willing obedience in their followers. Charles Darwin's observation that 'survival of the fittest' is what drives the natural world has sometimes been taken to mean that the possession of strength and power somehow overrides all moral considerations—that might is always right.

Even in the UK, a country that has thankfully escaped the domination of such evil authority figures so far, we can see that political leaders and others who, 50 years ago, might have been admired as models of behaviour persistently betray our trust. We begin to suspect that those in authority, with power to influence and control our lives, are focusing on their own advancement rather than the good of the people they are expected to serve with that power. Is it any wonder that we might reject this kind of authority and prefer to trust only ourselves?

Such disillusionment with authority applies also to many people's attitudes to the Church. As I suggested in Chapter 3, the Bible can be perceived by unbelievers as a book of oppressive rules, and the Church as an authority that wishes to impose those rules on others in order to take away their freedom of choice and bring them under control, perhaps for some sinister or manipulative purpose. Christians would, of course, argue against that view, but we have to admit that the abuse of power does sometimes take place in Christian communities. Among Christian believers, there have been those who have willingly accepted rigid authority structures within their church and discovered, to their cost, that their freedom to act according to their own conscience has been subtly undermined.

At the furthest extreme of religious (not necessarily Christian) abuse, news headlines occasionally tell shocking stories of communities of people who have been sucked into cults headed by leaders who demand unquestioning obedience to themselves and to the rules of the cult. The results can be tragic, as when 39 members of the Heaven's Gate group were found to have committed mass suicide in California in March 1997.

A related trend in our society is the increasing desire to bring our own circumstances, not just the lives of other people, under strict control. So, for example, we are sold a deluge of insurance policies, warranties and saving schemes that promise the end of fear for the future. We no longer seriously believe that science and technology can solve all our problems—we know that many scientific 'solutions' bring further problems in their wake—but our response to that realization is all too often to do all in our power to destroy what we cannot 'cure' and thus produce a perfectly predictable, secure, controlled world for ourselves to live in. We see this, perhaps, in the increasing offer of abortions to mothers expecting children with Down's syndrome and other incurable genetic or medical conditions.

So, are power and authority a force for good—peace, social cohesion and stability—or for terrible evil, mind-control, tyranny and destruction? What does the Bible have to say on the subject?

POWER TO BE FEARED

First and foremost, as the creator of the universe, God himself is the ultimate source of power and authority. His command to Adam and Eve to 'rule' over the rest of the created order (Genesis 1:28) suggests that human power and authority are delegated to us by God, but the Bible pulls no punches when demonstrating that human power and authority can be coveted for their own sake and used for evil purposes. The idea that 'might is right' is far older than Darwin, as can be seen in King Saul's fury at the sound of women praising David's military achievements over his own. On hearing the song, 'Saul has slain his thousands, and David his tens of thousands', Saul immediately assumed that David was, by virtue of his greater power, better suited to the kingship (1 Samuel 18:6–8). In addition, many of the most callous and wicked acts carried out by people in the Bible were rooted in the abuse of power: the enslavement and exploitation of the whole Hebrew nation by the Egyptian Pharaoh (Exodus 1—5), King Ahab's judicial murder of Naboth in order to obtain his vineyard (1 Kings 21:1–16) and King David's adultery with Bathsheba and murder of her husband Uriah (2 Samuel 11) all happened because the rulers involved thought that their high-ranking positions entitled them to trample over those weaker than themselves.

The early career of the Pharisee Saul shows that even a passion to do good can be corrupted when blind authority is used to destroy others. In his desire to keep the Jewish faith pure and free from the supposed heresy of the new Christian sect, Saul approved of the stoning of Stephen (Acts 8:1) and was 'breathing out murderous threats against the Lord's disciples' (Acts 9:1) shortly before his own dramatic conversion on the road to Damascus.

In the Old Testament especially, God's own unlimited power and authority are portrayed as the cause of awe and fear, and are beyond human knowledge and understanding (see, for example, Job 38—41). He has the ability and right to create or to destroy his creation as and when he chooses. The harrowing descriptions of his judgment on sin, in the story of the destruction of Sodom and Gomorrah (Genesis 19:23–25), for example, or in the prophecies of the fall of Jerusalem to the Babylonians (Jeremiah 4:13–31), show that God can and does reveal himself in a devastating fashion.

Another example of God's unrivalled power is seen in Elijah's contest with the prophets of Baal, when Elijah's brief and simple prayer to the God of Israel was answered with fire so ferocious that it consumed the sacrifice, wood, stones, soil, water and all (1 Kings 18:36–38). In the very next chapter of Elijah's story, however, we witness a much more gentle facet of God's nature as he reveals himself to the prophet not in the overwhelming forces of earthquake, wind and fire, but in a 'gentle whisper' (1 Kings 19:11–13).

POWER REINED IN

With the coming of Jesus, we find this gentler picture of the way in which God wields power gaining predominance. As we know, Jesus had supernatural power to heal diseases, work miracles with the forces of nature and raise the dead to life. Yet, it is notable that Jesus deliberately limited the scope of that power, acknowledging that he had it but choosing not to use it at every opportunity. For example, when Peter drew a sword on those who were arresting Jesus in the Garden of Gethsemane, Jesus rebuked him, saying, 'Do you think I cannot call on my Father, and he will at once put at my disposal more than twelve legions of angels?' (Matthew 26:53). Jesus chose in this situation to keep his undoubted power under wraps and allow himself to be taken away by the armed guards.

Even as he was dying, there were those among the observers who still half expected him to escape from the very jaws of death by some miraculous means: Mark 15:34–36 tells us that Jesus' cry of despair, '*Eloi, Eloi, lama sabachthani?*' was mistakenly thought to be a cry for rescue from the prophet Elijah. The expectation among his followers seems to have been, to the very end, that Jesus would become king of Palestine by using supernatural force to oust the Romans and liberate his people, the Jews. Presumably, Jesus would have had the power to do this, but he chose not to use it.

The key to this deliberate restriction of his power can perhaps be seen in the temptations that Jesus endured at the very beginning of his ministry, recorded in Matthew 4 and Luke 4. The three specific temptations—to turn stones into bread; leap from the top of the temple in order to prove God's protection; and worship Satan in return for the riches of the kingdoms of the world—were all to do with the use and potential abuse of his divine power. Jesus' refusal to use that power to meet his own physical needs or win followers by putting on some kind of sensational display of divine favour, or gain political ascendancy in the eyes of the world, set the tone for his whole ministry. Jesus had unlimited power that he could have used selfishly, for his own advancement, comfort and security, but he rejected all such avenues. Instead, he was determined to use that power only in the service of other people, continually living an unpredictable lifestyle, with 'nowhere to lay his head' (Luke 9:58).

Satan's taunt, 'If you are the Son of God...' in itself was a challenge to Jesus to prove his power simply for the sake of proving it. Jesus, though, resisted this approach, preferring instead to let himself appear powerless in the eyes of onlookers rather than flaunting his power in order to impress them—even to the point of allowing himself to be put to death in a shameful way.

UNDERSTATED AUTHORITY

If we look at Jesus' attitude to the use of authority (the right to act in a certain way, as opposed to the mere ability to do so), we find a similar story—but with a twist. There was one occasion when Jesus used an act of power to prove his authority. When four men lowered their paralysed friend through the roof of a house into the midst of a crowd, seeking miraculous healing, Jesus first proclaimed that the sick man's sins were forgiven and then healed the invalid's damaged limbs as a sign that he had the right to make that proclamation. On no occasion, though, is it recorded that Jesus felt the need to justify his authority verbally to those who demanded that he do so (see Mark 11:27–33 as an example).

In all his dealings with others—whether they were disciples, family members, people who came to him for healing or deliverance or his opponents—Jesus never made any attempt to prove himself or force his viewpoint on others by any form of argument or intimidation, or violate their free will by any kind of psychological manipulation. He mounted no campaign of persuasion to win followers, and neither did he choose his audience carefully to ensure a favourable response. He allowed all and sundry to approach him and let his simple but explosive teaching and actions speak for themselves. Onlookers could reject him or accept him freely, as they chose.

In his teaching and example to his disciples, Jesus also drummed home the principle that it is entirely unacceptable to 'pull rank' on other people or trample on their rights in order to force them to do what we want. In the upper room on the night of the last supper, Jesus and his disciples had every right to expect that a servant would wash their feet. Yet Jesus himself—the 'Teacher and Lord', the most important person in the gathering—chose to lay aside his authority and be the servant himself (John 13:4–15). On another occasion, when the disciples were arguing among themselves over which of them was 'the greatest', Jesus told them, '... the rulers of the Gentiles lord it over them, and their high officials exercise authority over them. Not so with you. Instead, whoever wants to become great among you must be your servant, and whoever wants to be first must be your slave' (Matthew 20:25–27). This principle of servant authority, which Jesus himself both taught and demonstrated, applies to every sphere of influence, in the Church and in secular society—it is the only model that really works.

AUTHORITY RECOGNIZED

Despite Jesus' unwillingness to impose his special rights and status as the Son of God on others, people did freely recognize that Jesus had authority like that of nobody else. They commented on a special quality in his teaching, which seemed to be rooted in first-hand knowledge of God's ways rather than relying on borrowed insights from other religious teachers (Matthew 7:28–29). More specifically, the Roman centurion who asked Jesus to 'just say the word', believing that his sick servant could be healed as a result, recognized that Jesus had authority to issue a command and see it obeyed (Matthew 8:8–9). The Syro-Phoenician woman who believed that her daughter could be delivered from demon possession with nothing more than the leftover 'crumbs' of Jesus' power showed a similar recognition (Matthew 15:27), and the occasion when Jesus calmed a storm on the Sea of Galilee with a word of command opened his disciples' eyes to the fact that he was no ordinary man (Mark 4:41).

After Jesus' death, the early Church, looking back, recognized that God had 'exalted him to the highest place' with a 'name that is above every name', not in spite of but because of the fact that he 'did not consider equality with God something to be grasped, but made himself nothing, taking the very nature of a servant...' (Philippians 2:6–7, 9). This free acknowledgment of Jesus' humility and authority over everything in heaven and on earth is at the heart of Christian belief.

Jesus demonstrated, in all he said or did, the fact that God deliberately and consistently subverts the world's ideas about power and authority—he turns them upside down and inside out, without fear that he will be in any way diminished in the process. After all, as Paul observes, 'God's weakness is stronger than human strength' (1 Corinthians 1:25, NRSV).

USE OF POWER IN THE *HARRY POTTER* STORIES

As you might expect in a story about the battle between good and evil, in which the two sides struggle for supremacy, the *Harry Potter* books have something to say about power and authority—their possession, use and abuse. As the story unfolds from the very first chapter, we are given to understand that power can be exploited recklessly for evil purposes or controlled and harnessed in the service of goodness, and authority can be used wisely and obeyed willingly or cause misery and oppression for those who come under its influence. There are four characters in particular who demonstrate different facets of these principles: Lord Voldemort, Barty Crouch Sr, Cornelius Fudge and Professor Albus Dumbledore.

Voldemort's overriding mission is to use his tremendous magical powers to conquer death for himself and pursue immortality (see *GoF*, p. 566) and he does not care how many other people he has to kill in order to achieve that personal ambition. After his revival in *The Goblet of Fire*, his proud boast to his gathered followers— '... I am now going to prove my power by killing [Harry Potter]' (p. 571)—shows that, to Voldemort, the idea that a powerful person has a moral obligation to restrain and harness that power would be unthinkable. At this stage in the story, Voldemort believes that Harry is no longer a threat to his purposes, so the desire to kill is quite gratuitous—a means only to 'prove' that he is able to do it— and Voldemort believes, in the words of his protégé, Professor Quirrell, that 'There is no good and evil, there is only power, and those too weak to seek it' (*PS*, p. 211). For Voldemort, to exercise restraint would give the appearance of weakness, and to appear weak is simply unbearable—he must be constantly exhibiting his dominance to those around about him, regardless of whether he is doing right or wrong.

By contrast, Barty Crouch apparently does believe in good and evil—a moral dimension to the use of power. As Head of the Department of Magical Law Enforcement during the time of Voldemort's first reign of terror, Crouch was known to be fiercely opposed to the Dark side of wizardry. However, as Sirius Black explains to Harry:

He's a great wizard, Barty Crouch, powerfully magical—and power-hungry... Crouch's principles might've been good in the beginning—I wouldn't know. He rose quickly through the Ministry, and he started ordering very harsh measures against Voldemort's supporters... Crouch fought violence with violence, and authorised the use of the Unforgivable Curses against suspects. I would say he became as ruthless and cruel as many on the Dark side. (GoF, pp. 456–457)

We might be reminded here of Lord Acton's famous words, 'Power tends to corrupt, and absolute power corrupts absolutely.' Like the apostle Paul before his conversion, Barty Crouch's zeal for goodness becomes subtly distorted into something ugly as he exercises power without mercy or self-control.

Cornelius Fudge, too, is corrupted by power, but that corruption shows itself most strongly in his terror that Dumbledore will use the return of Voldemort to make a bid for the position of Minister for Magic that Fudge himself currently holds. Because Fudge is power-hungry, he expects others to be so as well—just as King Saul assumed that the popular young warrior David must have his eye on the throne of Israel (1 Samuel 18). This dread of losing power leads Fudge to the wild speculation that Dumbledore is 'forming his own private army, with which he will be able to take on the Ministry of Magic' (OoP, p. 272). As Sirius explains to Harry, Ron and Hermione, 'Fudge thinks Dumbledore will stop at nothing to seize power. He's getting more paranoid about Dumbledore by the day'

(*OoP*, p. 272). The result of this paranoia is a whole year of misery for Harry and his fellow students at Hogwarts under the increasingly dictatorial rule of the Ministry-appointed DADA teacher Professor Umbridge—possibly the most sinister character yet created by J.K. Rowling.

Is Cornelius Fudge right to fear Albus Dumbledore? Certainly, Dumbledore is more than once described as the only wizard that Voldemort ever feared. We might assume from this that Voldemort, for one, credits Dumbledore with greater power than his own, as that is the only thing the evil wizard respects. Yet, in the opening chapter of *The Philosopher's Stone*, as Dumbledore and Professor McGonagall discuss the rumoured disappearance of the Dark Lord, Dumbledore modestly claims, 'Voldemort had powers I will never have.' McGonagall immediately retorts, 'Only because you're too—well—*noble* to use them' (*PS*, p. 14). This brief exchange clearly suggests a recognition by author J.K. Rowling that the deliberate restraint of power is a distinguishing mark of a good person.

It is not only Professor McGonagall who is aware of the full scope of Dumbledore's power. The house-elf Dobby, too, has heard that 'Dumbledore's powers rival those of He Who Must Not Be Named at the height of his strength' (*CoS*, p. 18). Yet, throughout most of the first four books in the *Harry Potter* series, we witness the Headmaster as a thoroughly approachable, jovial, gentle, ordinary person. If Dumbledore really is as powerful as people say, he shows no sign of wishing to prove it, like Voldemort, or of being in any way corrupted by it, like Crouch.

We might even be forgiven for thinking that all the talk about Albus Dumbledore having power on a par with the evil Lord Voldemort is nothing but hot air. Perhaps it's just propaganda, put about by the 'good' side in an effort to bolster their failing confidence? For the answer, we have to wait until the end of the fourth book—*The Goblet of Fire*—when Dumbledore, McGonagall and Snape have together burst into Professor Moody's office just in time to rescue Harry from death:

At that moment, Harry fully understood for the first time why people said Dumbledore was the only wizard Voldemort had ever feared. The look upon Dumbledore's face as he stared down at the unconscious form of Mad-Eye Moody was more terrible than Harry could ever have imagined. There was no benign smile upon Dumbledore's face, no twinkle in the eyes behind the spectacles. There was cold fury in every line of the ancient face; a sense of power radiated from Dumbledore as though he was giving off burning heat. (GoF, pp. 589–590)

Yes, Dumbledore has immense power, but he does not unleash it in full force for self-aggrandisement or to prove his dominance over others. He controls and restrains it, revealing its full force only when the evil he is opposing is of the deepest cunning and murderous intensity. This is J.K. Rowling's picture of the way in which power may be wielded in the cause of right by a supremely good person, and the picture is of a remarkably Christ-like character.

This may go some way to answering the concerns of Christians who fear that the young people most likely to be drawn into occult involvement by their love of the *Harry Potter* stories are those who feel powerless and vulnerable in their real lives. (In past decades, of course, the same kind of fear has been focused on the fantasy role-play game Dungeons and Dragons, and on heavy metal music, both popular with previous generations of young teenagers.) It has been suggested that people seeking affirmation and a stronger sense of identity for themselves may be encouraged by the story to pursue control and dominance over others by casting spells, for example (or simply claiming the power to cast spells). In fact, as the analysis above shows, there is nothing in the *Harry Potter* story itself that would lend support to any such idea. It remains the responsibility of the Church, however, to offer to everyone it contacts, especially the marginalized and those whose self-esteem has been knocked out of them by the cruelties of life, the kind of love that affirms people for their God-given individuality and human worth.

THE USE OF AUTHORITY IN THE *HARRY POTTER* STORIES

Albus Dumbledore does not have any kind of divine or supernatural authority in the way that Jesus Christ had (and neither does any other character in the story). However, as Headmaster of Hogwarts, Dumbledore has a large measure of secular authority conferred on him within the school. Once again, it is helpful to compare his use of authority with that of Barty Crouch—this time in relation to their treatment of servants.

Both Crouch and Dumbledore are employers of house-elves—small, magical creatures who act as domestic servants in large and/or wealthy wizarding households, usually unpaid and without holiday entitlement. There are certain rules governing the behaviour of house-elves in service: they may not use their own magic without their master's permission, they are not allowed to speak ill of their master and they are required to 'keep their master's secrets'. Unfortunately, these regulations make them easy victims for wizards who are prone to abuse authority. Crouch keeps a house-elf named Winky who, although loyal to a fault to her master and his family, is one day found in (illegal) possession of a wand that is proven to have conjured the Dark Mark—the sign associated with Voldemort and his followers (*GoF*, Chapter 9). As punishment, Crouch mercilessly sacks her, saying, 'I have no use for a house-elf who disobeys me' (*GoF*, p. 124). Most of the witnesses to this act feel, quite rightly, that Crouch has been unjust, but Percy Weasley backs him up with the words, 'A high-ranking Ministry official like Mr Crouch deserves unswerving obedience from his servants' (p. 137).

Ironically, Winky has indeed shown 'unswerving obedience' by colluding with Crouch in the terribly foolish act of harbouring a devoted servant of Lord Voldemort, Crouch's own son. She has kept his horrifying secret to crisis point, allowing Voldemort the chance to return to threaten the world again with his murderous plans. The relationship between Barty Crouch and Winky is, in fact, an example of the worst that can happen when a harsh, authoritarian leader is bolstered by a servant or follower who sacrifices all moral scruples (whether through weakness, misplaced loyalty or deliberate wickedness) and personal responsibility in favour of unquestioning allegiance. Winky is not a wicked creature. She believes she is doing right by fulfilling all the obligations laid on her as a house-elf, but she is foolish and obsessive in her devotion to her master, so she becomes a slave to evil, drawn into a web of corruption that threatens to destroy Winky herself as well as the many other people who suffer indirectly as a result of her collusion with Crouch.

We gain the impression from the story that most wizards who employ house-elves are likely to treat them harshly. The house-elf Dobby, whom we first meet in *The Chamber of Secrets*, also finds himself bound to serve an evil master, namely Lucius Malfoy. Despite the prospect of certain punishment, however ('Dobby will have to shut his ears in the oven door for this'), he does his best to warn Harry—without speaking ill of his master or giving away his secrets—that bad things are planned to happen at Hogwarts in the coming months. Dobby behaves more admirably than Winky in his determination to warn Harry of the danger that is about to confront him in the new school year, but his compulsion to punish himself for his disloyalty to his master, although it is presented comically in the story, shows him to be in mental turmoil.

At the end of the book, Harry tricks Lucius into setting Dobby free from his service. Dobby appears again in *The Goblet of Fire*. He has grown tired of 'freedom' and has taken employment in the Hogwarts kitchens, his new master being, of course, Albus Dumbledore. We soon discover that the terms of Dobby's employment are very different here. Not only does he have a pay-packet and regular holidays, but, most important of all, he is allowed to speak ill of his new master: 'He said we is free to call him a—a barmy old codger if we likes, sir!' Dobby confides to Harry (*GoF*, p. 332). Perhaps unsurprisingly, Dobby has no wish to call Dumbledore anything of the sort. He has been set free from slavery to an evil person and has freely chosen the role of servant to a good one. By complete contrast with Crouch's and Malfoy's regimes, there is no physical or mental danger involved for anyone who willingly obeys authority when it is used as Dumbledore uses it, with gentleness and openness, and for the good of the other person.

HUMILITY

Dumbledore's generous and humorous way of relating to his servants demonstrates one of his most outstanding qualities—humility. It is based on a deep inner security that eliminates any need to justify himself or parade his own 'greatness' before the rest of the world. It is this humility that allows him to pay full childlike attention to a sticky bag of sherbet lemons in the company of his deputy, Professor McGonagall (PS, p. 13), to give Dobby permission to call him a barmy old codger or, indeed, to express amusement at a newspaper report, by nasty journalist Rita Skeeter, that describes him as 'an obsolete dingbat' (GoF, p. 269).

Nowhere is his humility more clearly evident, however, than in the way he deals with Harry when he finds him in front of the Mirror of Erised. In a small but telling detail (unfortunately omitted from the Warner Brothers film Harry Potter and the Philosopher's Stone), J.K. Rowling describes Dumbledore slipping down from the table where he is perched to join Harry sitting on the floor as he explains the potential deceitfulness of our heart's desires. Here we have an old man with many titles and honours to his name (as shown on Hogwarts' headed notepaper), a wizard whose magical power is widely acknowledged to be second to none, sitting on the floor to comfort and counsel a single grieving child in the middle of a cold winter's night.

There is no sense that Dumbledore is in any way diminished by this act of love and service towards Harry—indeed, we gain the impression that he wouldn't care in any case. Just as his restraint of power is not seen as a sign of weakness, Dumbledore's use of his position of authority to serve other people rather than 'lording it' over them does not lead to any lack of respect from those who come under his influence (except for those such as Draco Malfoy and his cronies, who despise any sign of moral goodness). His authority is certainly recognized and freely acknowledged by the majority of his pupils and fellow teachers. So, when rumours of the deaths of Lily and James Potter are circulating at the beginning of *The Philosopher's Stone*, it is Dumbledore's confirmation of those rumours that Professor McGonagall seeks: '... whatever "everyone" was saying, she was not going to believe it until Dumbledore told her it was true' (*PS*, p. 14). Equally, in *The Chamber of Secrets*, it is Dumbledore's disapproval that Harry most dreads when it is discovered that he and Ron have arrived at Hogwarts by flying car rather than the more orthodox school train.

The most significant evidence for the very real potency of Dumbledore's authority in the school, though, comes near the end of *The Goblet of Fire*. I have already described in Chapter 5 how Dumbledore recognizes faux Moody as an imposter when Moody acts out of character, removing the injured and traumatized Harry from Dumbledore's sight. In fact, the crux of that out-of-character action is that faux Moody is disregarding a direct command from the Headmaster: Dumbledore tells Harry to stay where he is and Moody immediately helps Harry to his feet and leads him away. It is clear from this event that, despite his well-known weakness for sugar confectionery, his distribution of pay-packets and holiday entitlement to lowly house-elves and his refusal to demand the public respect that he deserves, Dumbledore expects to be obeyed when it really matters. His authority rests on humility and a willingness to serve other people, whatever their status, which means that those people in turn gladly submit to him.

IMPLICATIONS FOR TODAY

The society that J.K. Rowling depicts in her books is not a lawless one. Neither is it one where the tyrannical use of power, the arrogant handling of authority or unthinking submission to orders is condoned. Instead, her most admirable character, Professor

Dumbledore, combines humility and love with a complete lack of desire to prove the power and authority that he undoubtedly holds and is fully acknowledged by the people he serves. Meanwhile, other characters demonstrate the corruption that can so easily attach itself to someone when they abuse their power, and the harm that can be caused to other people as a result.

While secular and religious groups alike tend to demonstrate the abuse of power and authority more often than they do servant leadership, we find the stories of *Harry Potter*, yet again, pointing up aspects of attitude and behaviour that we, as members of the Church of Jesus Christ, should be modelling in reality to the rest of the world. All of us who find ourselves in a position of authority over other people, whether in the context of church ministry or secular organizations, have a serious responsibility to resist the many temptations that go along with that position and focus all our efforts on humble service to others. The ability to relinquish the drive for power and control and replace it with humility and an inner security that does not need to be justified or bolstered by other people's approval is, paradoxically, one of the most powerful forms of Christian witness that our world will ever see. Albus Dumbledore goes some way towards acting out the example set by Jesus himself, but readers of the *Harry Potter* stories will recognize that fact only if we Christians can match that standard in our everyday lives, in our shops, offices, schools, families and churches, continually pointing away from ourselves and towards Jesus in what we do.

CHAPTER 7

THE CHURCH'S RESPONSE

I will build my church, and the gates of Hades will not overcome it.
MATTHEW 16:18

Imagine that you are 13 years old, living somewhere in the UK. You've spent every spare moment in the last couple of months reading and re-reading the *Harry Potter* books and you think they are absolutely brilliant. You wonder what there might be on the Internet about them.

Talking of books, you were at assembly yesterday in school, where a visiting team came in and said what a great book the Bible is. It was a cool presentation, but if someone handed you a Bible now you wouldn't know where to find anything they talked about— Jesus or that guy Noah with his animals. Was Noah around at the same time as Jesus or not?

You know how to surf the web, though. This is what you feel comfortable with. You log on to the web and type into your search engine "Harry Potter". The first five of about 900,000 websites are listed on the screen in front of you. You choose to see the next 100 entries, then the next 100. You're clicking on a few that look interesting and, suddenly, before your eyes there is a tirade of abuse. You can see at a glance that it's saying things about Harry that are complete rubbish—just lies—and that it's something to do with Christianity. There's a load of stuff about witches being stoned to death, but it's all in that weird old-fashioned language that religious people use where every other word ends in 'eth', so you don't take much notice. By the time you've finished reading, you're so shocked and angry you're practically in tears. With a few swear words about religious nutcases, you shut down the PC and settle into a fifth reading of *Harry Potter and the Prisoner of Azkaban*—your favourite. You'll have another look at some of the websites for Potter fans another day, but you'll steer clear of anything that looks as if it might be by witchcraft-obsessed 'Christians'. As for that lot who came to school yesterday, perhaps, you think, they wouldn't look so good if you found out everything they really believed.

We know that the issues surrounding the *Harry Potter* books have been hotly debated within the Church, with passionate views on both sides, but what effect has the anti-Potter campaign had on the Church's witness to those outside it? In these days of Internet communication, we Christians can no longer talk among ourselves without being 'overheard'. As I said in the Introduction, my first inkling of the opposition to Harry came not from my local church but a website accessible within about five clicks of a mouse to every PC owner in the world. Many non-Christian readers of the *Harry Potter* books are well aware of the kind of criticisms being expressed, too. In the Internet discussion forum of which I'm a member, comprised mainly of American and British fans, the Church's opposition has been debated regularly and at length. Not once have I heard of a non-Christian *Harry Potter* fan who has been encouraged to investigate the claims of Jesus Christ as a result of reading the Church's criticisms. Instead, a typical reaction is initial shock and bewilderment, followed by genuine grief, which changes to anger that then hardens into a resistance to Christianity—a resistance that may not have been there before. The anti-Harry furore has done nothing to advance the cause of the gospel; instead, it has had, as far as I can see, an entirely negative effect on people's perceptions of our faith.

By far the most damaging element of the campaign is the fact that so many of the protestors have provided false information on the *Harry Potter* books and so many more have taken that false information on trust, without testing its validity. As I suggested in Chapter 1, simple factual errors, misinterpretations and distortions based on short quotations taken out of context have been combined with blatant untruths (such as the claim that there are no acts of self-sacrifice in the story), confusing and misleading those who have not read the original sources. When those who absorb the false-hoods go on to base their own protests on the things they have read and heard, rather than first-hand knowledge of the books them-selves, the problems are compounded. According to a *Daily Mail* article on the filming of *Harry Potter and the Philosopher's Stone* at Gloucester Cathedral,[35] none of the leaders of a small group of Christians planning a protest outside the cathedral had read the books. When a report like this appears in a national newspaper, it must cause the Church to lose credibility in the eyes of those outside the faith. What a contrast with Jesus himself, who was recognized to speak with authority because he knew first hand about the kingdom of God.

At its worst, this combination of false information with naïve trust has led to a tendency in some Christians to swallow the most outrageous claims about the *Harry Potter* books without question. One e-mail spoof that has been circulated in churches, warning of the dangers of the books, includes a blasphemous and obscene 'quotation' supposedly taken from an interview given by J.K. Rowling to *The Times* newspaper. The content of the e-mail actually originates in a satirical Internet magazine, which was poking fun at Christians who believe that the *Harry Potter* stories lead children to reject the Bible in favour of witchcraft. How the original writers must have laughed to discover that the satire itself had been taken seriously by those same Christians they were making fun of, and how doubly gullible the Church must appear to them as a result!

When the apostle Paul told the Thessalonian church to 'test everything' (1 Thessalonians 5:21), he was warning them against believing everything taught to them in the name of God. I would apply this warning to everything spoken about the *Harry Potter* books from within the Church (including this book!). As believers in God, who is devoted to truth, the first question for us to ask when reading any comment, whether for or against Harry, must be 'Is it true?' It does not take hours of closeted prayer or any special gift of spiritual discernment to test the truth of something like the hoax mentioned above. My own test involved a quick and easy search through the Internet archives of *The Times*, which revealed that the supposed interview with J.K. Rowling never took place. Thankfully, over 300 others have made direct enquiries on the subject to the newspaper itself, as shown by a copy of a letter from *The Times* published on the Internet.[36]

It is crucial to the Church's witness that we are seen to be committed to telling the truth and analysing questions of right and wrong from a position of knowledge rather than ignorance. If Christian leaders are perceived by the secular world to be unable or unwilling to tell the truth about a work of children's fiction, they can have no hope of credibility as preachers of the truth of the gospel.

Such neglect of the vital importance of truth—telling and testing—is not the only damaging aspect of the anti-Potter campaign. I believe that many of the concerns expressed by those who vehemently oppose the *Harry Potter* stories are symptomatic of a general attitude that needs to be challenged—one that relates to the interface between the Church and those who are outside it. What should be the relationship between Christians and secular society? How does the Church fall short of the calling of God in its dealings with the non-Christian world?

In his prayer for his disciples in the upper room, Jesus talked of their being in the world, but not of it (John 17:15–16). Earlier, in his Sermon on the Mount, he described his followers as being like salt and light in the world (Matthew 5:13–14). Salt has several uses—it can act as a preservative, melt ice and enhance the flavour of food. As Christians, we should remember Jesus' analogy and be preventing decay in our society, melting cold hearts so that they're receptive to the gospel and bringing spiritual 'flavour' to our sometimes bland and boring environment. To delve deeper into the comparison, if salt is to succeed in preserving meat, it has to be rubbed well into the fibres; it can melt ice only when its molecules combine fully with those of the water; and the full flavour of our vegetables or chicken casserole comes out only when the salt dissolves into the water or gravy. In other words, salt has to be absorbed fully into its surroundings before it can do its job. In the same way, we Christians have to be absorbed fully into our society before we can make a scrap of difference.

Over the last few decades, however, we have been intent on building an alternative Christian subculture in order to protect ourselves from the evil of the world with 'safe' parallel activities. So we have Christian music, Christian novels, Christian education, Christian television and radio, even Christian keep-fit tapes and Christian holiday accommodation, which we keep to ourselves with no real hope or expectation that our non-Christian friends (if we have any) will ever wish to join us in enjoying them. It is possible for us to be sure of spending the bare minimum of time outside the cushioned environment of the Christian ghetto, completely separated from the world outside, which soon comes to be perceived as a place of fear and danger. The effect of this sharp division between Christian and non-Christian culture is that the Church becomes light shining behind blackout curtains and salt inside a blocked salt-cellar—in other words, exactly the opposite of what Jesus himself said we should be.

In the context of the debate about the *Harry Potter* books, I see this attitude expressed in two ways, which are actually two sides of the same coin. First, there is a desire to 'ban' the books as unfit reading material for people in the Church, and replace it with 'Christian' literature, which cannot be found in secular bookshops. This immediately puts a barrier between Christian youngsters and their peers, and begins to breed in them, too, the ghetto mentality of fear and suspicion.

Second, and even more depressingly, I have seen many

expressions of a desire to distance the *Harry Potter* stories from the truly great fantasy writings of C.S. Lewis and J.R.R. Tolkien, Christian writers whose works have 'salted' the secular market for decades and whose themes have sometimes been compared with J.K. Rowling's. Many non-Christian young *Harry Potter* fans go on to read the *Narnia Chronicles* and *The Lord of the Rings* simply because they have been told of the similarities between these books and the *Harry Potter* stories and yet so many Christians fall over themselves to deny any connection, thus undermining a golden opportunity to encourage unchurched young people to explore the works of authors who had a deliberate intention to promote Christian ideals.

Even more powerful than Jesus' words about salt and light is his prophecy to Simon Peter, after Simon's famous affirmation of him as the Son of God. In response, Jesus said to him, '... you are Peter, and on this rock I will build my church, and the gates of Hades will not overcome it' (Matthew 16:18). This is a picture of hell under siege, the gates barred to withstand a full-scale assault from the Church of Jesus Christ. Yet, so often, Christians speak and act as if the roles are reversed, as if the Church is being besieged by the powers of Satan and all his marauding hosts and is about to fall. So the cry goes up to retreat, get behind the walls, raise the drawbridge and stay there, desperately trying just to survive for as long as possible, perhaps until Jesus gallops in to take us 'home'.

The truth is that Satan is the one who is defeated, holed up in fear and trembling, shooting his fiery darts from behind the ramparts of his fiercely defended strongholds. Ephesians 6:16 encourages us to extinguish them with the shield of faith and move on. Yet, we have Christians whose sole focus seems to be to discern the strategies of Satan, learn as much as possible about his plans of attack and encourage the Church to defend itself. Others keep a watch for signs of the approach of Judgment Day, like fearful sentries scanning the horizon for any faint hope of rescue from an un-endurable enemy assault.

With regard to the *Harry Potter* books, this is where the occult 'experts' come into their own, exhorting us to be fully aware of the many ways in which spiritual darkness operates, educating us in their perception of the unfettered power of Satan. Jesus did not initiate his disciples into the secrets of witchcraft. Although he gave a broad overview of the devil's character—that he is a liar, thief and murderer (John 8:44; 10:9)—his overriding priority was to teach about the values and strategies of the kingdom of God, not the kingdom of Satan. Even when he sent out 72 workers to preach and they returned in high excitement at the experience of casting out demons, Jesus deliberately redirected their focus, saying, '... do not rejoice that the spirits submit to you, but rejoice that your names are written in heaven' (Luke 10:20).

Most of the New Testament letter writers, too, while remaining fully aware of the spiritual conflict, continually and passionately urge their readers to pursue holiness with its numerous facets. Peter, to take but one example, says, '... make every effort to add to your faith goodness; and to goodness, knowledge; and to knowledge, self-control; and to self-control, perseverance; and to perseverance, godliness; and to godliness, brotherly kindness; and to brotherly kindness, love. For if you possess these qualities in increasing measure, they will keep you from being ineffective and un-productive in your knowledge of our Lord Jesus Christ' (2 Peter 1:5–8). Paul identifies for us the fruit of the Spirit, with its nine 'flavours'—love, joy, peace, patience, kindness, goodness, faithful-ness, gentleness and self-control (Galatians 5:22–23)—while his famous chapter on love sets the highest possible standard for us to achieve (1 Corinthians 13).

If we are truly aspiring to cultivate all of these Christian characteristics, we will have enough on our plates to absorb all our energies our whole lives long. We will have no time to waste on exploring the secret strategies of Satan, and we do not need to know them in order to defeat him. The Bible tells us that if we wish to be effective in our Christian lives, we need to possess Peter's list of virtues 'in increasing measure'. Certainly, poring over explanations of occult numerology in order to remain 'aware' of Satan's supposed influence on children's literature may be superficially more exciting than the daily, dogged pursuit of brotherly kindness, but the latter will enhance our witness to the people of our acquaintance, the former will not.

In his book *People of the Lie*, M. Scott Peck quotes from Aldous Huxley's *The Devils of Loudun*:

Those who crusade not for God in themselves, but against the devil in others, never succeed in making the world better, but leave it either as it was, or sometimes even perceptibly worse than it was, before the crusade began. By thinking primarily of evil we tend, however excellent our intentions, to create occasions for evil to manifest itself. [37]

As I suggested earlier, those who crusade against other people's enjoyment of the *Harry Potter* stories do not succeed in encouraging those people to explore the wonders of Christianity; they merely raise barriers in their minds that prevent them from even wishing to know more about Jesus. Throughout this book I have reached the conclusion that the *Harry Potter* stories point away from the assumptions of our current secular, postmodern society and towards key aspects of Christian attitudes and behaviour. In particular, the character of Professor Albus Dumbledore, J.K. Rowling's 'epitome of goodness', has emerged as the linchpin of every one of those 'sub-Christian values', to use C.S. Lewis' phrase again. Dumbledore is the one who most clearly states the principle that we are personally responsible for our choices between good and evil; who arouses hope and generously offers grace to those who need it; and who is a source of inspiration and strength for Harry in his fierce battle against evil. Dumbledore sets the example of devotion to truth and realism, and his humble willingness to serve others with the power and authority vested in him puts him head and shoulders above those who wish only to assert themselves and destroy other people.

In every way, Professor Dumbledore is the standard to which Harry and his friends aspire within the story, and his goodness is recognized and admired by countless readers in the real world as well. As followers of Jesus Christ, however, we have a real-life role model, source of inspiration and, indeed, saviour, who far surpasses Albus Dumbledore, and it is our responsibility to make him known in words and actions to the people round about us. Those who complain even about the good qualities in the *Harry Potter* books— on the grounds that they are not linked with an acknowledgment of the Christian God—need to recognize that it is not the job of a secular novelist to preach Christianity. That task falls to the Church—both its clergy and its laypeople—and it is to the Church's shame that the non-Christians who yearn for the virtues they find in the *Harry Potter* books do not seem to be able to recognize those virtues in the message that we in the Church are claiming to preach. If such goodness is more apparent in a fantasy novel than in the Church of today, it is an indictment of the Church, not the author of the fantasy.

This is the most urgent question for the Church to answer: why are millions of people intrigued by the *Harry Potter* stories and indifferent to—even ignorant of—the claims of Christianity? Instead of crusading against the devil in the *Harry Potter* stories, the Church needs to crusade for God in itself. We must turn the spotlight on ourselves, to explore prayerfully why we currently seem unable to communicate to our world the message of hope, grace, responsibility for choice, victorious goodness, truth and servant authority that are reflected in Albus Dumbledore and brought to full reality in Jesus Christ. Part of the answer must surely be that we need to take seriously the difficult task of remaining absorbed in the world, without being squeezed into its mould, developing Christ-like characters that will consistently demonstrate the power and grace of God.

All people, whether they acknowledge the Christian God or not, are created in his image, and the doctrine of common grace asserts that, for this reason, all people display something of his goodness and partake in his blessing. Centuries ago, John Calvin (1509–64) commented:

Whenever we come upon these matters in secular writers, let that admirable light of truth shining in them teach us that the mind of man, though fallen and perverted from its wholeness, is nevertheless clothed and ornamented with God's excellent gifts. If we regard the Spirit of God as the sole fountain of truth, we shall neither reject the truth itself, nor despise it wherever it shall appear.[38]

I believe that we should neither reject nor despise the truths that are everywhere to be seen in J.K. Rowling's stories. Rather, we should engage with them, and with other people who love her books but do not (yet) love Jesus Christ, talking about the characters and themes in a way that encourages further thought and discussion. A shared knowledge and enjoyment of the stories might open up many opportunities for stimulating conversations with unbelievers about the big issues of life and death. Most people would be reticent to discuss the deepest desire of their hearts or their greatest fears, except with their closest friends. Pose the question 'What would you see in the Mirror of Erised?', though, or 'What would your Boggart be?' and the very same issues become easier to broach. 'Repentance' might sound like a nasty, religious word, but if the discussion topic is to do with possible motives for Professor Snape renouncing the service of Lord Voldemort and allying himself with Dumbledore's cause, the subject starts to seem closer to home. The choice between 'what is right and what is easy'; the victory of hope over fear and despair, or truth over illusion and falsehood; the seductiveness of power and the power of self-sacrifice; and above all, the conviction emerging loud and clear in *The Order of the Phoenix*, that love conquers all—the minds of readers of the *Harry Potter* books are open to all these concepts. How open are we, though, to the possibility that God, in his grace, can and will use these ideas to lead these readers closer to an understanding of his Kingdom and his ways?

I hope and pray that, in the years to come, God's grace will be seen to have been at work in those who are enraptured by Harry's story today.

NOTES

1. C.S. Lewis, 'Christianity and Culture', in *Christian Reflections*, ed. Walter Hooper, Fount, 1981, pp. 39–40

2. David Wilkinson, *The Power of the Force: The spirituality of the Star Wars films*, Lion, 2000, p. 10

3. Penelope Lively, *The Driftway*, Heinemann, 1972

4. Richard Adams, *Watership Down*, Rex Collings Ltd, 1972

5. C.S. Lewis, *Out of the Silent Planet*, The Bodley Head, 1938, ch. 22

6. Charles Colson, *Breakpoint Commentary 91102*, 2 November 1999, www.pfmonline.net/transcripts

7. Alan Jacobs, *First Things*, issue 99, January 2000 (copyright © 2000 *First Things*)

8. Anonymous spokesman, 'What's Wrong with Harry Potter?', formerly at www.freedomvillageusa.com

9. Berit Kjos, 'Bewitched by Harry Potter', www.crossroad.to/text/articles/Harry9-99.html

10. Richard Abanes, *Harry Potter and the Bible*, Christian Publications Inc., 2001

11. Nick Pollard, *Why Do They Do That?*, Lion, 1998, p. 110

12. C.S. Lewis, *Mere Christianity*, Geoffrey Bles, 1952, p. 76

13. *Mere Christianity*, p. 76

14. John Houghton, *A Closer Look at Harry Potter*, Kingsway, 2001, pp. 55–56

15. *A Closer Look at Harry Potter*, p. 66

16. *A Closer Look at Harry Potter*, p. 56

17. Francis Bridger, *A Charmed Life*, DLT, 2001, pp. 67–73

18. Connie Neal, *What's a Christian to Do with Harry Potter?*, Waterbrook Press, 2001, pp. 167–176

19. Robert W. Jenson, in 'How the World Lost its Story', *First Things*, issue 36, October 1993 (copyright © 1993, *First Things*)

20. Lindsey Fraser, *Telling Tales: An Interview with J.K. Rowling*, Mammoth, 2000, pp. 15–16

21. C.S. Lewis, *The Lion, the Witch and the Wardrobe*, Geoffrey Bles, 1950 (Fontana pbk edition p. 76)

22. J.R.R. Tolkien, *The Lord of the Rings*, George Allen & Unwin, 1954–55. For prophecy, see *The Fellowship of the Ring*, HarperCollins pbk edition p. 324. For name 'Estel', see *The Return of the King*, Appendix A, HarperCollins pbk edition p. 414

23. Peg Kerr, 'Seven Heavenly Virtues: Hope'; see under files/Essays at http://groups.yahoo.com/group/HPforGrownups

24. Interview with Ann Treneman, *Sunday Express*, 2 July 2000

25. Karen Jo Gounaud, Family Friendly Libraries Book Report 'Should *Harry Potter* Go to Public School?', October 1999

26. C.S. Lewis, *The Screwtape Letters*, Geoffrey Bles, 1942 (Fount pbk edition pp. 73–74)

27. Bob Geldof, *Is That It?*, Penguin, 1986, p. 271

28. *Is That It?*, pp. 281, 282

29. *The Lion, the Witch and the Wardrobe*, p. 148

30. C.S. Lewis, *Voyage to Venus*, The Bodley Head, 1943, ch. 14

31. J.K Rowling, *Fantastic Beasts and Where to Find Them*, Bloomsbury, 2001

32. M. Scott Peck, *The Road Less Travelled*, Arrow Books, 1978, p. 52

33. M. Scott Peck, *People of the Lie*, Arrow Books, 1983

34. Rex Mason, *Jeremiah*, The People's Bible Commentary, BRF, 2002

35. *Daily Mail: Weekend*, 21 October 2000

36. Letter from *The Times* regarding satirical interview at www.gospelcom.net/apologeticsindex/p03.html

37. Aldous Huxley, *The Devils of Loudun*, Harper & Row, 1952, p. 192, quoted in *People of the Lie*, p. 301

38. John Calvin, *Institutes of the Christian Religion*, I, quoted in Leland Ryken, *Triumphs of the Imagination*, IVP USA, 1979, p. 161

★★★★★ ALSO FROM BRF ★★★★★

FAITH ODYSSEY

A JOURNEY THROUGH LIFE

RICHARD A. BURRIDGE

To boldly go where no Christian book has gone before... *Faith Odyssey* takes us on a journey from the ashes of sorrow to shouts of gladness, from slavery to freedom, from being lost to coming home. As we make the journey, passages from the Bible are placed alongside stories drawn from a wide range of literature, TV and film, from Homer's *Odyssey* to *2001: A Space Odyssey*, from *Star Trek* and *Star Wars* to *The Lord of the Rings* and *The Matrix*, mixing *Narnia*, *Harry Potter* and *Pilgrim's Progress*.

How do we get to the start? Whom will we meet along the way? And how can we make it our journey?

ISBN 1 84101 317 X   £7.99

Available from your local Christian bookshop or direct from BRF using the order form on page 144.

See the *Faith Odyssey* website: www.faithodyssey.net

THE SUBVERSIVE MANIFESTO

LIFTING THE LID ON GOD'S POLITICAL AGENDA

JONATHAN BARTLEY

God has a political agenda—and it's a subversive one, according to this book which lays down a radical challenge for Christians to rediscover the political dimension of their faith. All too often we stick with 'private' readings of scripture, failing to realize the power contained in its amazing stories and ideas. In fact the Bible presents a faith that is wider and more exciting than we realize—a faith that can change not only people's hearts but also the way societies are run, economies are structured, and legal systems organized.

With illustrations drawn from the author's experiences in the 'corridors of power', this book combines an innovative interpretation of the Bible with challenging ideas for applying it to everyday life.

ISBN 1 84101 211 4   £7.99

Available from your local Christian bookshop or direct from BRF using the order form on page 144.